THE WILTON SCHOOL

Decorating Cakes

A REFERENCE & IDEA BOOK

CREDITS

Creative Director Richard Tracy

Supervising Editor Zella Junkin

Cake Designer Steve Rocco

Senior Cake Decorator Susan Matusiak

Cake Decorators Mary Gavenda
Nancy Suffolk Guerine
Judy Wysocki
Diane Knowlton

Editor Jeff Shankman

Writers Ann Jarvie
Mary Enochs
Marita Seiler
Mary Ann Cuomo

Project Manager Cathy Franczyk

Production Manager Laura Fortin

Production Coordinator Mary Stahulak

Art Director Frani Marek Janci

Photography Peter Dean Ross

Set Designer Carey Thornton

Wilton Industries, Inc., 2240 W. 75th Street, Woodridge, IL 60517
www.wilton.com

Wilton Industries, Canada Ltd., 98 Carrier Drive, Etobicoke, Ontario M9W 5R1 Canada
Phone (416) 679-0790, Fax (416) 679-0798, e-mail: wiltncan@Interlog.com

Wilton Industries/ Europe, Inc. Unit 8 Axis/Hawkfield Business Park, Whitchurch, Bristol BS14 0BY England.
Phone 011-44-1179-465777, Fax 011-44-1179-465888

For photography purposes, many cakes in this book were decorated (by right- and left-handed decorators) with royal icing.

Printed in Italy

Library of Congress Catalog Card Number: 98-75344

Dear Friend,

Wilton has been teaching people the fun of cake decorating for more than 50 years. It all started at The Wilton School, where a small class in a Chicago kitchen has grown into the world's leading resource for baking and cake decorating. Even today, the techniques Wilton teaches are based on lessons first developed at The Wilton School. Now, *Decorating Cakes* presents many of these popular baking and decorating techniques to help you create wonderful cakes for all your celebrations.

Decorating Cakes is a reference book you can keep by your side whenever you decorate. All the fundamentals of cake decorating the Wilton way are here—star and shell borders, beautiful roses, fondant and more—shown step by step, just as a Wilton instructor would. This book is ideal for beginners who want to practice and perfect each technique. It is also a great resource for experienced decorators who need a quick review or new decorating inspiration.

Once you know the basics, you can put them to work on the great selection of cakes in this book. You will then be ready to explore other Wilton idea books for the perfect cakes to please your family and friends.

We at Wilton hope that you will use *Decorating Cakes* often for many years of happy decorating.

Vince Naccarato

Vincent Naccarato
President

CONTENTS

GETTING PREPARED

TECHNIQUES & BORDERS

FLOWER MAKING

FONDANT

MORE TO KNOW

SPRING FLOWER BASKET

Instructions on page 96.

Getting Prepared

Before you can start decorating, you need to think about the fundamentals. Beautifully baked cakes, icing of perfect texture and color, plus a good collection of baking and decorating tools are essential to your decorating success. In this section, we'll give you the information you need to get started. Once you learn the basics, you'll be ready to explore specific decorating techniques with confidence.

Tools

Having the right tools on hand really does make all the difference. Using a professional decorating bag and tip, for example, is the only way you can create intricate stringwork and lifelike icing flowers. A turntable really does improve decorating speed. Angled and straight spatulas? A must! To get you started, we're providing this checklist of the best tools, accessories and ingredients most commonly used by decorators. You'll find many of these essential decorating supplies in the Wilton Products section, starting on page 104. Or look for the current edition of the annual *Wilton Yearbook of Cake Decorating*, for a complete list of Wilton products.

Cake Preparation

You must start with a quality **Baking Pan** in order to bake a cake with a perfect decorating surface. There are many good baking finishes to choose from, such as non-stick, anodized aluminum and insulated. Just be sure to select a durable pan which won't warp, rust or chip during repeated use.

Several **Cooling Grids** in various sizes are invaluable for the decorator. They're not just for cooling—grids help to release the cake from the pan without damage. You'll also use them when pouring icing over cakes. For a pretty presentation of your cake, you can use **Cake Boards** wrapped with **Colored Foil** or an elegant **Cake Plate**. Cake boards are available in rectangles and rounds in sizes to fit your cake—they can also be cut to fit any shaped cake.

Once your cake is baked, use a **Cake Leveler** to cut off crowns and to torte into equal sections for filling. For easier decorating, we suggest placing your cake on a **Turntable Cake Stand**—it puts you in perfect decorating position with an easy turn.

Tools and Supplies for Icing

When preparing your icing, you have lots of options. Of course, you can make your own icing using the recipes in this book. Many ready-to-use icings or icing mixes are available—but be sure they will be of the proper consistency for the decorating you want to do. Follow package instructions for use. (Most ready-to-use icings are meant for spreading, not decorating. **Wilton Decorating Icing** is the proper consistency for decorating). For royal icing, you will need **Meringue Powder** to make decorations dry hard. **Piping Gel** is transparent gel which can be tinted any color for decorating or writing; it adds a shimmering effect to your cakes. **Icing Flavorings** such as butter, vanilla and almond, are also handy to have. For decorating, clear extracts are best—they add taste without adding color.

It's vital to use **Concentrated Icing Color** to tint your icing. Mixing in a large amount of liquid color will change the consistency of icing, making decorating difficult. Concentrated color lets you add less color in your icing. Many colors are available, including pastel shades. Colors can be mixed to achieve almost any shade.

Spatulas are used for icing cakes, filling decorating bags, color blending and more. An 11-12 inch spatula gives you greater control when icing larger cakes. An angled, 8-10 inch spatula is perfect for icing the tops of cakes and is easier to use when filling decorating bags.

Choose the right decorating bag for your needs. **Featherweight Bags** are lightweight polyester which is flexible and reinforced for strength. They are used with a **Coupler** when more than one tip is needed for the same color icing. **Disposable Bags** are strong, flexible plastic which can be used with or without a coupler—excellent for melting candy wafers too. **Parchment Paper Triangles** are suggested when tip changes are not called for, especially for small amounts of icing. They are best for brush striping where icing color could stain a polyester bag.

Decorating Tips have openings specifically cut for certain shapes and sizes of decorations (see pages 110-113). Your cake instructions will list which tips you need. A good starting assortment would be round tips 3 and 12, star tips, 16, 18 and 21, basketweave tips 47, leaf tips 67 and 352, petal tip 104 and drop flower tip 2D. A **Cake Icer Tip** #789 is especially valuable to have—its very wide opening lets you ice a cake quickly with a uniform finish. To attach a tip to your bag when you want to use multiple tips, you will need **Tip Couplers**. The base goes inside the bag to hold the tip in place, while the ring twists around the base to attach the tip. Just twist off the ring to change tips.

You can add pretty contoured effects to an iced cake using a **Decorating Triangle or Comb**. Just run the edge against the icing to form ridges.

Pipe certain icing flowers, such as roses or daisies, on a **Flower Nail**. It's shaped like a nail, with a wide head to hold the flower and a long stem to turn as you pipe. Attach a waxed paper square with icing to the nail for easy removal of each flower. Keep a set of **Decorator Brushes** for a variety of decorating needs. Use them for striping bags, painting designs on cakes, attaching fondant flowers with water and more.

A **Practice Board Set** is a new decorator's best friend. It includes a reusable decorating board and technique patterns for convenient practice. A clear overlay lets you decorate over each pattern for borders, figures, drop flowers, writing and printing.

Many other decorating products are available. See page 76 for Fondant products. A wide selection of decorating products may be ordered by calling Wilton Mail Order at 800-794-5866 or purchased from your Wilton Dealer.

Other Tools from Your Kitchen

When you're mixing different colors of icing, have several Stainless Steel or Glass **Mixing Bowls** on hand. Choose a 4 quart size to handle most icing needs and a 1 1/2 quart size for mixing smaller amounts of color. To keep icing fresh and at the right consistency, use **Air-Tight Plastic Containers**.

You will use **Waxed Paper** quite often during decorating. It's essential for holding and positioning flowers made on the Flower Nail and also for tracing and transferring patterns. **Aluminum Foil** is another kitchen staple decorators keep handy; use it to wrap cakes for freshness, to line Lily Nail Flowers and to cover cake boards. To cut these wraps, you'll need a good pair of **Scissors**—use them also for removing buttercream flowers from the nail and trimming plastic dowel rods and lollipop sticks to size.

More little things you will need: **Toothpicks** for marking cakes, drawing patterns in icing and adding color to icing; **Clean Damp Cloths**—essential for keeping hands and decorating tools clean and for covering freshly mixed icing until ready to use. And if you are going to be a decorator, look the part—wear an **Apron** to protect your clothing.

Icing

Using the proper icing, made to the correct consistency, is essential for beautiful decorating. Flowers, for example, generally require a stiff icing—otherwise, they may droop. Borders look better with a medium-stiff consistency that will hold the shape and show the detail of a shell or a star. Writing or leaves require a slightly thinned consistency that will flow well from the tip. Icing that can peak to an inch or more is stiff; less than that is considered medium consistency. Icing that flows easily from a tip without running is a thin consistency.

In this section, we've listed general descriptions of icings, their uses, qualities and consistency. Use this information, along with the chart on page 94, to determine the right icing for your cake. And refer to our icing recipes on pages 92 and 93.

Buttercream Icing – Best Tasting, Most Versatile

Buttercream is one of the most popular icings for many reasons. You can do so many things with buttercream—from covering the cake to piping borders, flowers and most decorations. Buttercream is also very easy to make and to manage. You can adjust its consistency with a little liquid or added confectioners' sugar, making it stiff enough to create perfectly-defined flowers or thin enough for writing messages. Everyone loves the rich flavor of buttercream; it's the best tasting of all the decorating icings. The creamy texture means flowers remain soft enough to be cut with a knife.

There are three types of buttercream decorators commonly use. Each of these creates a thin-to-stiff consistency, depending on the amount of corn syrup or confectioners' sugar added (sugar stiffens):

Basic Buttercream is great for most decorating. It has an excellent texture for icing cakes smooth, piping shell or star borders, for figure piping and for flower making, including roses and sweet peas.

Snow-White Buttercream yields truer colors than Basic Buttercream Icing, because there's no butter used in the recipe. The pure white color of this icing makes it ideal for wedding cakes. Snow-White Buttercream also will crust over slightly, due to the meringue powder used in the recipe. This crusting means flowers can be air dried and easily transferred to the cake.

Wilton Decorator White Icing is ready for spreading or decorating, right out of the can. Its pure white quality helps you achieve deep, true color when you add any icing color. Decorator White is excellent for most decorating.

Royal Icing – Dries Hard for Long-Lasting Decorating

Only royal icing, made with meringue powder, dries hard enough for flowers and intricate decorations to last indefinitely. Once hardened, if properly stored, the decorations never soften or crumble. This means that a busy decorator can make many flowers in advance—and when you're making up to 300 flowers for a wedding cake, working ahead is crucial.

Royal icing has a very sweet flavor—you'll use it less for its taste than for its "indestructible" quality. It has a thin-to-stiff consistency depending upon the amount of water added. You will also use royal icing as the "glue" for attaching decorations, for figure piping and for decorating cookies and gingerbread houses.

When preparing royal icing, keep all bowls and utensils grease-free; any grease will break down the icing. During decorating, cover the icing with a damp cloth to prevent crusting.

ICING COMPARISONS

Two pretty ways to decorate floral cakes. At left, an all-fondant design highlighted by roses and drapes. At right, a buttercream cake topped with full ruffles and royal icing carnations made in advance.

Icing Quantity Guide

PAN SHAPE	SIZE	QUANTITY IN CUPS*
ROUND	6"	3
	8"	4
	9"	4½
	10"	5
	12"	6
	14"	7¼
	16"	8¾
SQUARE	6"	3½
	8"	4½
	10"	6
	12"	7½
	14"	9½
	16"	11
HEART	6"	2/2
	9"	4½
	12"	5¾
	15"	8¾

* Approximate Quantity Needed to Ice and Decorate 2 Layers with border

Smooth, Satiny Coating – Fondant

Fondant makes a cake surface smoother and shinier than any other icing. It provides an immaculate surface, great for coating all kinds of cakes because its thick consistency seals in freshness. There are two types of fondant used by decorators:

Rolled Fondant has a denser, more dough-like texture than other icings. This makes it ideal not only for coating your cake, but for cutting, molding and modeling many decorations. Knead the fondant first, then roll out as you would a pie crust before applying. It's easy to then lift the fondant sheet up and place it on your cake, or to cut shapes for decorating. Because rolled fondant keeps cakes fresh, it's a great choice for bridal cakes which must be made in advance. You may use the fondant recipe on page 93 or Wilton Ready-To-Use Rolled Fondant.

Quick-Pour Fondant pours and dries to a semi-hard, very smooth and shiny surface. It's meant strictly for coating, and works well on most cakes, petit fours and cookies. Does not work on sponge-type cakes.

Other Icings

Wilton Whipped Icing Mix has a velvety texture that is great for spreading on cakes, piping most decorations and topping many desserts. Unlike most whipped toppings, it holds its shape very well, letting the decorator make stars, shells and even roses. It has a light, delicate flavor, available in chocolate or vanilla; the vanilla yields any color. Use chocolate when you need black icing that will taste good.

Stabilized Whipped Cream Icing uses piping gel to make it stiffer than ordinary whipped cream, so you may use it for piping borders and writing. It has a light, thin-to-medium consistency that stays soft on your decorated cake when refrigerated; use it immediately after mixing. Yields pastel colors.

Fluffy Boiled Icing creates a light, airy texture for smooth flowing decorations and luxurious iced cakes. It's ideal for borders, figure piping, writing and stringwork. Use immediately. Yields bright or pastel colors.

Wilton Tube Icings give decorators a convenient, easy way to add color. Great for decorating small areas of your cake without having to mix a new color icing. Made to fit standard Wilton Decorating Tips using a standard coupler, which allows you to decorate any technique.

Color

Color is as basic to your decorating as the icing and the cake. Choosing appropriate colors for your cake will help you capture just the mood you want for the occasion.

When planning your cake, think about color. Gather inspiration from the theme of your celebration. The icing colors you choose will carry that theme and personalize your decorating. Look around, notice everyday objects—from a garden in bloom, to the clothes people wear. Which colors appeal to you? Use your favorite colors in your decorating.

Don't be afraid to try something different. Have fun using rich, bright colors or different color combinations. Begin by making a monochromatic cake, decorated all in white or in a single, pale color. Try using color decorations in contrast to an all-white cake background. Decorate using all pastels or all primary colors. Experimenting with color will help you decide which colors work to make your cake designs spectacular!

The designs below use the same basic techniques to create a perfect cake for any occasion. You can simply tailor your colors and toppers to the event—from a child's birthday to an intimate wedding.

SWEPT UP IN ROMANCE
Instructions on page 96.

SPRAY OF DAISIES
Instructions on page 96.

JUST FOR DAD
Instructions on page 96.

HAPPIEST CLOWN IN TOWN
Instructions on page 96.

Mixing Color In Icing

Begin with white icing and use concentrated icing color which will not affect your icing consistency. Using standard food colors can thin down your icing and affect your ability to pipe certain decorations. If you are tinting icing dark brown or black, begin with chocolate icing—your icing will not have the aftertaste that large amounts of these icing colors may produce. If you are tinting a large area red, use No-Taste Red.

Dip a toothpick into the color, then swirl it into the icing. Add color a little at a time until you achieve the shade you desire. Always use a new toothpick each time you add color; you want to avoid getting icing into your jar of color. Blend the icing well with a spatula.

Consider the type of icing you are using when mixing color. Icing colors intensify or darken in buttercream icing about 1-2 hours after mixing. Royal icing requires more color than buttercream icing to achieve the same color intensity.

Always mix enough of any one icing color for your entire cake. For example, if you are going to decorate a cake with pink flowers and borders, color enough icing for both. It is difficult to duplicate an exact shade of any color, an important fact if you want to keep color consistent on the cake.

Blending Colors

You can create just about any color you want, using the right combination of icing colors, in the right amounts. With proper blending, you will duplicate team colors, company logos and more.

Practice mixing small amounts of icing first to produce the special color you desire. Use these guidelines, but don't be afraid to experiment!

NEW COLOR:	Navy Blue =	Warm Gold =	Raspberry =	Maroon =	Hunter Green =	Aqua =	Chartreuse =
Base Color	Royal Blue +	Golden Yellow +	Burgundy +	Red-Red +	Kelly Green +	5 Parts Sky Blue +	9 Parts Lemon Yellow +
Plus this Color	Sm. Amount of Black	Touch of Brown	Red-Red	Black	Sm. Amount of Black	1 Part Leaf Green	1 Part Leaf Green

Bag Striping Effects

You can easily pipe exciting two-tone decorations just by adding a different color inside the bag before you put in your tinted icing. This way, you can pipe flowers with natural light and dark tones or a rainbow-colored clown suit to brighten up the party.

Brush Striping produces more intense multiple colors because it is done with straight icing color brushed into the bag. Apply one or more stripes of icing color with a decorating brush, then fill the bag with white or pastel-colored icing. As the icing is squeezed past the color, decorations will come out striped.

Spatula Striping produces two-tone and realistic pastel tones in flowers and figure piping. It is done with pastel-colored icing, striped inside the decorating bag with a spatula. After striping, fill the bag with white icing or another shade of the same color as the striping. Squeeze out decorations with soft contrasts.

Decorating Tips & Bags

The Decorating Bag is the container that holds the icing and tip together so that you can create all sorts of beautiful decorations. There are three types of bags from which to choose. Select the bag type that is most suited to your project or preference: Featherweight Bags, in strong polyester, offer durability and size variety. Disposable Plastic Bags provide the ultimate in clean-up convenience. And Parchment Bags are ideal for smaller amounts of icing, highlighting, color striping techniques and easy clean-up. All three bag types may be used with or without a Tip Coupler, which simply enables you to quickly change tips without having to change the bag.

Using a Tip Coupler

The photo at right illustrates how bag, tip and coupler fit together. See pages 16-17 for instructions on cutting bag and fitting tip.

The Tip Coupler BASE fits INSIDE the bag before filling with icing

The Decorating Tip is placed over the part of the BASE extending from the bag

The Coupler RING is twisted on over the tip to lock it in place

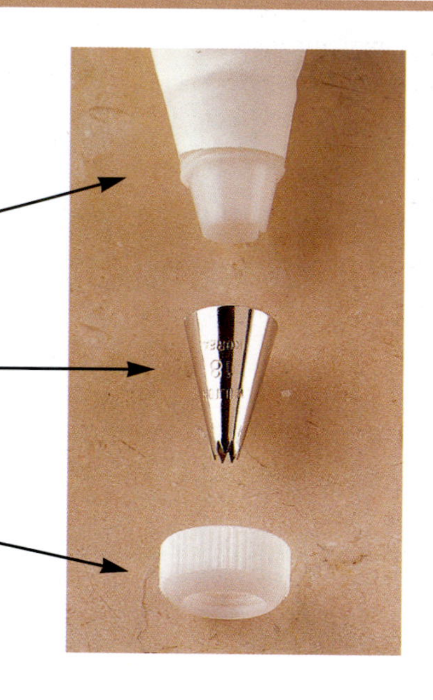

Change Decorating Tip by twisting off the RING, changing tip, then replacing RING.

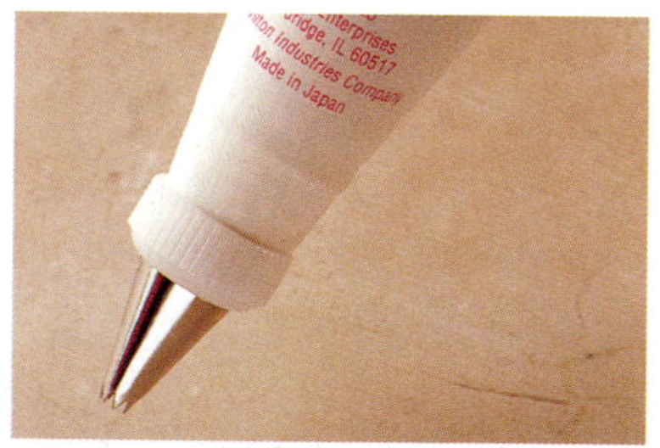

Standard Coupler

Most standard size decorating tips will use a standard coupler. As a general rule, standard tips have a $^3/_4$ inch base diameter. If your tip has a larger diameter, use the large coupler or no coupler at all.

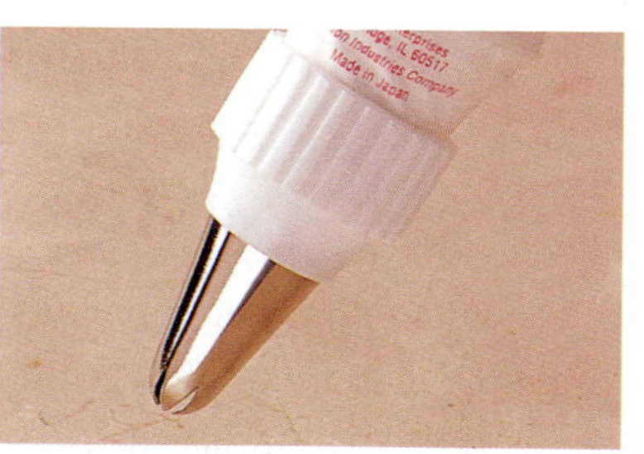

Large Coupler

These tips use large couplers: 1A, 2A round; 2010 triple star; 234, 235 multi-opening; 4B, 6B, 2110 star; 113, 115, 366 leaf; 1B, 1C, 1E, 1F, 1G, 2C, 2D, 2E, 2F drop flower; 116, 121, 123, 124, 125, 126, 127, 402, 406 ruffle; 2B basketweave; 250, 252 specialty.

Without Coupler

Some tips are sized to be used without a coupler. 1D basketweave; 789 cake icer; 127D giant rose; 403 ruffle; 190, 194, 195 drop flower; 112 leaf; 172 open star; 8B, 1L round; 134 multi-opening. Use these tips with any decorating bag, simply drop the tip into the bag and trim the bag accordingly.

Tips

This is where all decorating begins. Tips by the score help you produce your favorite techniques—lifelike floral arrangements, intricate lacework, bold shell borders, basketweave designs and more!

These small metal cones are shaped to produce various designs when icing is pressed through them. The size and shape of the opening on a decorating tip identifies the basic group, or family to which the tip belongs and determines the type of decorations the tip will produce. Within each family, each tip will produce an effect somewhat similar to that of the other tips in the family.

Take a look at these families and some of their decorating possibilities on pages 110-113. Notice the characteristic openings on each family and the variety of designs each will produce.

Round tips are used for outlining details, filling and piping in areas, writing and printing messages, figure piping, dots, balls, beads, stringwork, lattice and lacework, vines, flower centers and floral work. These tips are smooth and round.

Multi-string tips pipe rows and clusters of strings, beads, scallops, even grass and hair!

Star tips produce the most popular decorations—deeply grooved shells, stars, fleur-de-lis, rosettes and flowers. The most popular star tips used are numbered 13 through 22.

Leaf tips create perfect floral enhancements. The v-shaped openings of these tips give leaves pointed ends. With any leaf tip you can make plain, ruffled or stand-up leaves.

Drop Flower tips make pretty one-squeeze flowers—these are the easiest flowers for a beginning decorator to do. The number of cuts on the end of the tip determines the number of petals the flower will have. Each drop flower tip can produce two different flower varieties—plain or swirled.

Ruffle tips have a teardrop-like shaped opening that yields ribbons, swags, bows, streamers, scallops, ruffles and special effects.

Basketweave tips are wonderful for woven designs. These decorating tips have a smooth side for making smooth, wide icing stripes and/or one serrated side for making ribbed, wide icing stripes.

Rose tips have an opening that is wide at one end, narrow at the other. Using rose tips you can make a variety of petals that form flowers like the rose, carnation, daisy, pansy and more.

Specialty tips add a totally different look! This family includes tips with very distinctive design. Use them to make ring candleholders, deeply ridged shell borders, Christmas trees, hearts, three-dimensional and ridged ruffles.

Economically-priced decorating tips are a great way to challenge your decorating abilities and experiment with new designs—you'll be amazed at the decorations you can produce. Select a handful and have some fun!

Where to Begin

Begin with your basic group of tips—round tips 3 and 12, star tips 16, 18 and 21, basketweave tip 47, leaf tips 67 and 352, rose tip 104 and drop flower tip 2D. A good collection of tips would also include a range of sizes in each family. It's also a good idea to have several of those tips you use most often, so that you don't have to clean a tip each time you change icing color. Refer to our tip chart on pages 110-113 for further information.

Metal tips can be used with decorating bags of any kind. All standard size decorating tips can be used with a Wilton standard coupler. A coupler is a two-piece device that fits onto your decorating bag and holds the decorating tip in place. It's a great convenience when you want to change decorating tips without changing bags, such as when you are using different tips with the same color icing. The coupler base goes inside the cut bag to hold the tip in place, while the coupler ring twists around the base on the outside of the bag to attach the tip. Just twist off the ring to change tips.

Standard tips can also fit on Wilton Tube Icings when a coupler is used. Tube Icings give the decorator a fast way to add small amounts of color to a cake.

Care and Storage

Your decorating tips must be designed for precision and durability. Wilton tips are made of non-rusting, nickel-plated brass. Their seamless design and finely-cut openings will help create precision decorations. The optimal way to store decorating tips is upright, on pegs. This protects the finely cut ends from being bent out of shape. With proper care and storage, your decorating tips will last a lifetime!

To keep tips in perfect decorating condition, wash after each use in hot, soapy water. Rinse in hot, clear water. If bits of icing clog the opening, gently use a tip brush to clean icing away. Air dry, or if using immediately, dry with a soft towel.

Bags at a Glance

Featherweight Bags are made of flexible, reusable polyester—just wash in the dishwasher or in hot, sudsy water after each use. They are specially coated to prevent any seepage of grease and remain your most durable choice for decorating. Available in sizes from 8 to 18 inches.

Disposable Bags are made of clear plastic and are designed to be discarded after each use. They're great for saving you clean-up time—giving you more time to practice decorating. These bags are grease-resistant and flexible. Great for melting and piping Candy Melts® wafers. Available in 12 inch size only in packs of 12 and 24.

Parchment Bags are bags you make from parchment triangles. These disposable bags are usually used for smaller amounts of icing, flowing in color flow icing, color striping techniques and melting and piping Candy Melts® wafers. They are your most economical choice of decorating bags. Just use them once and toss. Available in 12 and 15 inch sizes.

Preparing a Featherweight or Disposable Bag

1. Remove ring from coupler base. Drop the coupler base, narrow end first, into the bag and push it down as far as you can.

2. Featherweight Bags: using a pen or pencil, mark the spot on the outside where the bottom screw thread (closest to tip) is outlined against the bag material. Disposable Bags: mark a spot on the outside that is 1/4 inch BELOW the bottom screw thread.

3. Push the BASE up into the bag so that you can cut an opening at the mark.

4. Push the BASE down through the opening. One thread should be showing. Place a Decorating Tip over the part of the BASE extending from the bag.

5. Put the RING over the tip and twist it on, locking the tip in place.

Filling and Closing the Bag

1. While holding the bag with one hand, fold down the top with the other hand to form a generous cuff over your hand as shown.

2. With an angled spatula, fill the bag with approximately 1/2 cup of icing. It is important not to overfill the bag; otherwise, icing may squeeze out the wrong end.

3. Remove icing from the spatula by squeezing the bag with your thumb and fingers against the spatula and pulling the spatula out.

4. Close the bag by unfolding the cuff and twisting the bag closed. This forces the icing down into the bag.

"Burp" the bag, or release air trapped in the bag, by squeezing some of the icing out of the tip into the icing bowl just before decorating the cake.

"Burp" the bag after each refilling.

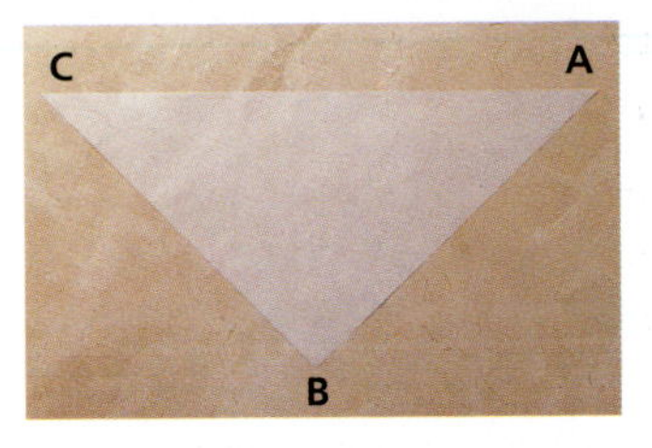

1. Note that the points of the triangle have been labeled A, B and C in the photo. Place the triangle on a flat surface with the B facing you.

2. Curl A up and under, bringing it toward you until points A and B meet. The curled edge from A should lie on top of the edge between C and B as shown.

3. Hold points A and B together with your left hand, picking up C with your right. Wrap C around to meet A and B in back. All three points should align to form a sharp point.

4. Hold the bag with both hands, thumbs inside, and slide A and C in opposite directions to make the upside- down "W" as shown.

5. Fold the points of the bag down into the bag. Then refold to secure. Tape the outside seam of the bag if desired.

6. To use a Decorating Tip without a Coupler, cut 3/4 inch off the end of the bag, then drop the tip in, narrow end first. Don't be concerned if the tip doesn't fit snugly; the icing will hold it in place.

7. To use a Tip Coupler, drop the BASE, narrow end first, into the bag and push it down as far as you can. Holding the coupler and bag together in place with one hand, twist on the RING. When secure, tear away the tip of the parchment bag. Unscrew the RING, position the Decorating Tip on the Coupler and replace the RING, locking the tip into place.

Filling and Closing the Parchment Bag

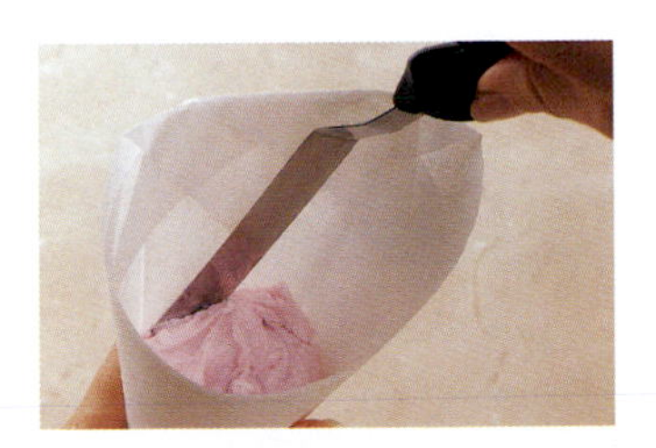

1. Hold the bag near the bottom and fill the bag only half full with an angled spatula using about three tablespoons of icing at a time.

2. Remove icing from the spatula by squeezing the bag with your thumb and fingers against the spatula and pulling the spatula out.

3. Close the bag by first squashing the top of the bag flat above the icing.

4. Fold in left side, then right side, then the top. Hold the bag just above the fold to prevent icing from coming out of the top of the bag.

Cake Preparation

Think of your cake as the canvas on which you will create beautiful icing decorations. To achieve the masterpiece you want, it is essential that your canvas be smooth and free of crumbs. These steps to preparing and icing your cake will result in a perfectly smooth decorating surface for your work of art.

Baking

Follow recipe directions for recommended batter amounts and specific baking instructions for the pan size you choose. Hint: To help cakes rise high, add 1 to 2 tablespoons Wilton Meringue Powder Mix to each boxed two-layer cake mix.

Prepare the pan by generously greasing the inside with a pastry brush or paper towel and solid vegetable shortening. For best results, do not use butter, margarine or liquid vegetable oil. Spread the shortening so that all indentations are covered. Sprinkle about 2 tablespoons of flour inside the pan and shake so that the flour covers all greased surfaces. Turn pan upside down and tap lightly to remove excess flour. If any uncovered spots remain, touch up with shortening and flour. Pour batter into pan and place in preheated oven.

After cake has baked the specified time, remove it from the oven and let it cool in pan on rack for 10 minutes. Run a thin knife between the cake and side of the pan. Unmold from pan by placing cooling rack against cake and turn both cooling rack and pan over. Lift pan off carefully. Cool at least one hour before icing. Brush off loose crumbs.

Leveling

After the cake has cooled at least one hour, you'll need to level the top of the cake. This can be done in one of two ways.

Using a Serrated Knife
Place the cake on a circle board, then place the board on a Wilton Trim 'n Turn Decorating Turntable.

While slowly rotating the stand, move the knife back and forth across the top of cake in a sawing motion to remove the crown. Try to keep knife level as you cut.

Using the Wilton Cake Leveler
Position the ends of the cutting wire into the notches at the desired height.

With legs standing on the work surface, cut into the crusted edge using an easy sawing motion, then proceed by gently gliding through the cake.

Torting

A serrated knife or the Wilton Cake Leveler also may be used to cut a cake into multiple layers. Torting adds extra height, drama and taste to the cake when the layers are filled with icing, pudding or fruit filling.

Using a Serrated Knife
Measure cake sides and mark with dots of icing or toothpicks all around. Place one hand on top of the cake to hold it steady and rotate the stand.

While slowly turning the cake, move the knife back and forth to cut the cake along the measured marks. Repeat for each additional layer.

Using the Wilton Cake Leveler
Torting is easily accomplished with the Wilton Cake Leveler. Simply follow the same directions as for leveling.

Separating the Layers
Carefully slide the top torted layer onto a circle board to keep it rigid and safe from breakage. Repeat for each additional layer to bottom.

Filling the Layers

Fill a decorating bag with medium consistency icing and use a large round tip, like tip 12. Or simply use the coupler without mounting a tip.

Starting with the bottom layer, leveled side up, create a dam or circle of icing just inside the edge of the cake. Creating a dam is an effective way of preventing the filling from seeping out when the layers are replaced. To create the dam, squeeze a circle about 3/4 inch high and 1/4 inch from the outside edge.

Fill the dam with icing, preserves or pudding.

Place the next layer on top, making sure it is level. The weight of the layer will cause the circle of icing to expand just right. Repeat until all layers, except the top, are assembled.

Place the top layer leveled side down, so the top of the cake is perfectly smooth and level.

Icing the Cake

Using a Spatula

The trick to keeping crumbs out of your icing is gliding your spatula on the icing—never allow it to touch the surface of the cake. Place a large amount of thin consistency icing on the center of the cake top. Spread across the top, pushing toward edges.

Cover the sides with icing. Smooth sides first by holding the spatula upright with the edge against the side, slowly spinning the turntable without lifting the spatula from the cake's surface. Return excess icing to the bowl and repeat until sides are smooth.

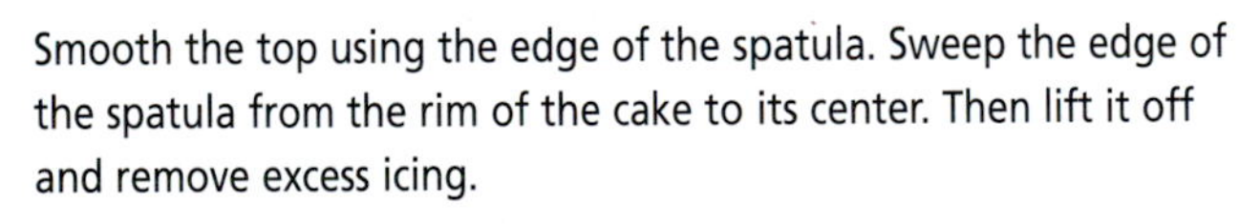

Smooth the top using the edge of the spatula. Sweep the edge of the spatula from the rim of the cake to its center. Then lift it off and remove excess icing.

Rotate the cake slightly and repeat the procedure, starting from a new point on the rim until you have covered the entire top surface.

Smooth the center of the cake by leveling the icing with the edge of your spatula. For easier smoothing, it may help to dip the spatula into hot water, wipe dry and glide it across the entire surface. Set the cake aside and allow the icing to crust over for at least 15 minutes before decorating. At this point you may also lay Wilton Parchment Paper on the iced cake top and gently smooth with the palm of hand.

Using the Wilton Icer Tip

Trim a 16 inch Featherweight bag to fit tip 789. Fill bag half full with icing. Hold bag at 45° angle and lightly press tip against cake.

Squeeze a ribbon of icing in a continuous spiral motion to cover cake top, with last ribbon forcing icing over edge of cake top.

To ice the sides, squeeze icing as you turn the cake slowly. Repeat the process until the entire cake side is covered. Smooth the sides and top with a spatula, same as above.

SWEPT UP IN ROMANCE

Instructions on page 96.

Techniques & Borders

Your icing turned out great—now you're ready to learn to pipe beautiful shapes on your cake. Stars, shells, dots, lines and other techniques are the foundation of your decorating knowledge. We'll tell you step-by-step how to pipe each one, including the angle, pressure and movement to use for a uniform look. With practice, you can build on these basics to create many other impressive designs and borders.

Three Essentials of Cake Decorating

Every decoration you make is the result of three things working together: the consistency of your icing; the position of the bag, that is, the way you are holding it and the amount and type of pressure you apply to the bag. You'll know when you have everything right because you'll get perfect results time after time. This will take practice. The more you concentrate on perfecting these three essentials, the sooner you will achieve perfect results.

1. Icing Consistency

If the consistency of your icing is not right, your decorations will not be right either. Just a few drops of liquid can make a great deal of difference in your decorating results. Many factors can affect your icing consistency, such as humidity, temperature, ingredients and equipment. You may need to try using different icing consistencies when decorating to determine what works for you. As a general guideline, if you are having trouble creating the decorations you want and you feel your icing is too thin, add a little more confectioners' sugar; if you feel your icing is too thick, add a little more liquid. In royal icing recipes, if adding more than 1/2 cup confectioners' sugar to thicken icing, also add 1-2 additional teaspoons of Meringue Powder.

Stiff icing is used for decorations such as flowers with upright petals, like roses, carnations and sweet peas. Stiff icing also creates your figure piping and stringwork. If icing is not stiff enough, flower petals will droop. If icing cracks when piped out, icing is probably too stiff. Add light corn syrup to icing used for stringwork to give strings greater elasticity so they will not break

Medium icing is used for decorations such as stars, borders and flowers with flat petals. If the icing is too stiff or too thin, you will not get the uniformity that characterizes these decorations. Medium to thin icing is used for icing your cake. Add water or milk to your icing recipe to achieve the correct consistency.

Thin icing is used for decorations such as printing and writing, vines and leaves. Leaves will be pointier, vines will not break and writing will flow easily if you add 1-2 teaspoons light corn syrup to each cup of icing.

2. Correct Bag Position

The way your decorations curl and point and lie depends not only on the icing consistency but also on the way you hold the bag and the way you move it. Bag positions are described in terms of both angle and direction.

ANGLE

Angle refers to the position of the bag relative to the work surface. There are two basic angle positions, 90° (straight up) and 45° (halfway between vertical and horizontal).

The angle in relation to the work surface is only half the story on bag position. The other half is the direction in which the back of the bag is pointed.

DIRECTION

Correct bag direction is easiest to learn when you think of the back of the bag as the hour hand of a clock. When you hold the bag at a 45° angle to the surface, you can sweep out a circle with the back end of the bag by rolling your wrist and holding the end of the tip in the same spot. Pretend the circle you formed in the air is a clock face. The hours on the clock face correspond to the direction you point the back end of the bag.

The technique instructions in this book will list the correct direction for holding the bag. When the bag direction differs for left-handed decorators, that direction will be listed in parentheses. For example, when a bag is to be held at 3:00 for a right-handed decorator, it should be held at 9:00 for a left-handed decorator.

One more thing: since most decorating tip openings are the same shape all the way around, there's no right side and wrong side up when you're squeezing icing out of them. However, some tips, such as petal, basketweave, ruffle and leaf have irregularly shaped openings, and for those you must watch your tip position as well as your bag position. If the tip opening must be in a special position, the instruction will tell you.

90° angle, or straight up, perpendicular to the surface. Used when making stars, flat flowers or rosettes.

45° angle, or half way between vertical and horizontal. Used for writing and borders.

Back of Bag at 3:00

Back of Bag at 6:00

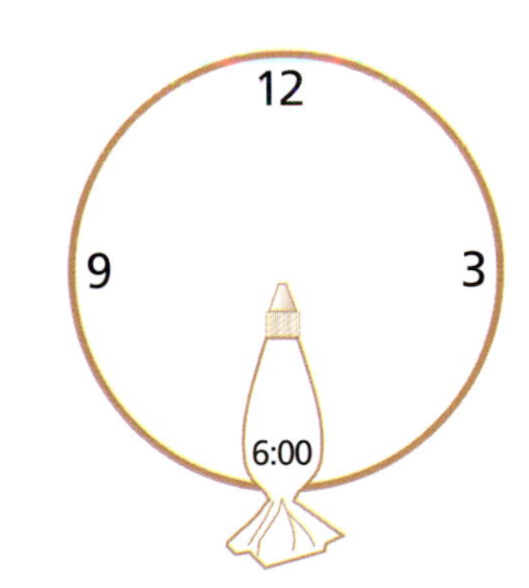

Bag Direction with clock position

3. Pressure Control

In addition to having the proper icing consistency and the correct bag position, you'll need to master three types of pressure control: heavy, medium and light. The size and uniformity of your icing design are affected by the amount of pressure you apply to the bag and the steadiness of that pressure. In other words, how you squeeze and relax your grip on the decorating bag. Your goal is to learn to apply pressure so consistently that you can move the bag in a free and easy glide while just the right amount of icing flows through the tip. Practice will achieve this control.

Heavy Pressure Control | Medium Pressure Control | Light Pressure Control

Star

Practice with Tip: #16

Icing Consistency: Medium

Bag Position: 90°

Hold Tip: Between 1/8 and 1/4 Inch Above Surface

1. Hold the decorating bag straight up, with the tip between 1/8 and 1/4 inch above the surface, while using your other hand to hold the tip steady.

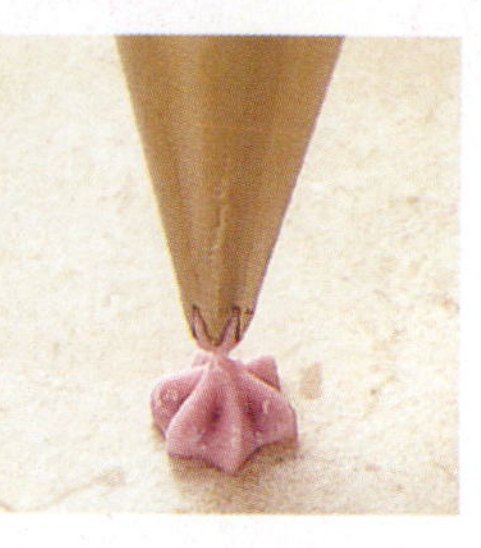

Squeeze the bag to form a star. Increasing or decreasing the amount of pressure changes the size of the star.

2. Stop squeezing the bag completely before you lift the tip from the star.
3. Lift the tip up and pull away from your piped star.

Pull-out stars add even more dimension to your cake. To make them, hold bag at a 45° angle to surface. As you squeeze out icing, pull tip up and away from cake. When your mound is high enough, stop pressure and pull tip away. Work from bottom to top of area to be covered with pull-out stars.

Dot

Practice with Tip: #3

Icing Consistency: Medium

Bag Position: 90°

Hold Tip: Slightly Above Surface

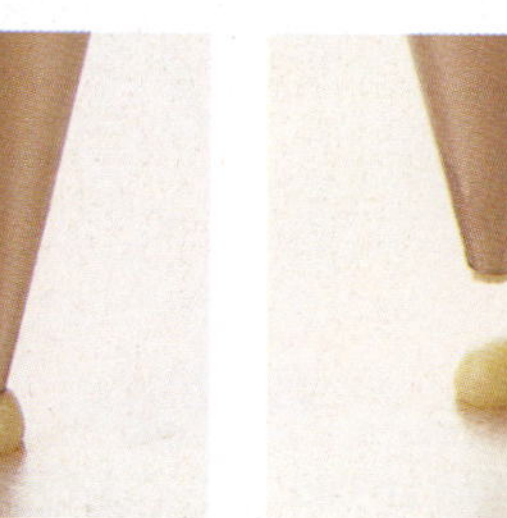

1. Hold the bag straight up with the tip slightly above the surface. Squeeze the bag and keep point of the tip in icing until the dot is the size you want.

2. Stop squeezing the bag completely before you lift the tip from the dot.

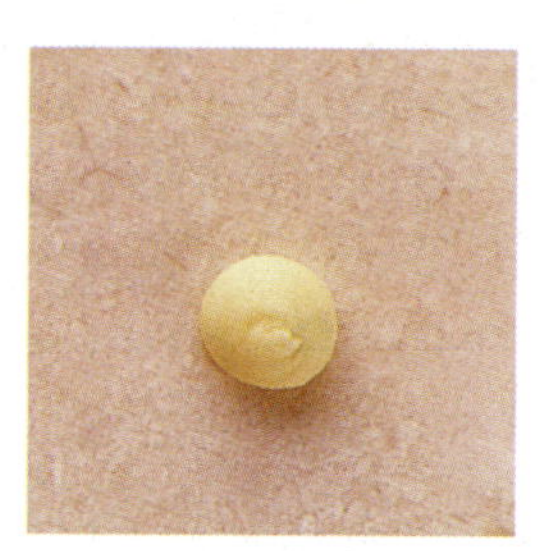

3. Lift the tip up and pull away from your piped dot.

Popular for its simple design and many uses! Pipe dots for flower centers, faces, figure piping and border effects. When making large dots, lift the tip as you squeeze to allow icing to fill out completely.

Ball

Practice with Tip: #9

Icing Consistency: Medium

Bag Position: 90°

Hold Tip: Slightly Above Surface

1. Squeeze the bag, applying a steady even pressure. As the icing begins to build up, raise the tip with it, but keep the tip end buried in the icing.

2. Stop squeezing as you bring the end of the tip to the surface.

3. Lift the tip up and pull away from your piped ball. Use the edge of the tip to shave any point so that your ball is nicely rounded.

An important technique to master, the ball shape makes bold borders, and is a step-up technique to figure piping. Vary the basic look by adding stars, dots or spirals on the ball shapes.

CELEBRATION OF STARS

The combination of piped star flowers with fresh star-shaped flowers makes for a beautifully balanced presentation. Instructions on page 97.

CASCADING CLUSTERS

Drop flowers are simple to do but they can be arranged in so many pretty ways. Gathered in clusters, they add impact to this fluffy iced cake. Instructions on page 97.

Picot

Practice with Tip: #1L

Icing Consistency: Thin

Bag Position: 90°

Hold Tip: Slightly Above Surface

1. Pipe three small dots in an even horizontal line.

2. Pipe two dots below top row, between spaces.

3. Pipe one dot below second row to form a triangle shape.

Fine, delicate designs piped onto a cake are commonly referred to as "embroidery". Although some embroidered designs can be rather complex, the simple elegance of picot is easily achieved in freehand with a series of small, easy-to-pipe dots.

Star Drop Flower

Practice with Tips: #2D, 3

Use Large Coupler

Icing Consistency: Medium for Flower, Thin for Center

Bag Position: 90°

Hold Tip: Slightly Above Surface

1. Hold the bag straight up, with the end of drop flower tip 2D just touching the surface.

2. Squeeze, letting the icing build up to make the flower. Stop squeezing, then lift the tip away.

3. Make a tip 3 dot flower center, holding your bag straight up and keeping the tip buried as you squeeze. Stop squeezing, then pull your tip up and away.

Pipe them in buttercream when you want to add pretty flowers instantly, right on your cake. Use royal icing if you want to make them in advance. Star drop flowers are the easiest flowers to make because the tip does all the work.

Swirl Drop Flower

Practice with Tips: #2D, 3

Use Large Coupler

Icing Consistency: Use Royal Icing. Medium for Flower, Thin for Center

Bag Position: 90°

Hold Tip: Slightly Above Surface

1. Turn your wrist in toward you before piping. Hold bag straight up, just touching the surface. You will turn wrist a full twist. Starting with the flat of your knuckles at 9:00 (3:00), as you squeeze out the icing, slowly turn your hand, with knuckles ending at 12:00.
2. Stop squeezing and lift the tip away.

3. Make a tip 3 dot flower center, holding your bag straight up and keeping the tip buried as you squeeze. Stop squeezing, then pull your tip up and away.

For a fancier drop flower, just twist your wrist! The swirled look adds a nice motion effect to the cake. You must squeeze and turn at the same time—keep practicing this movement.

Shell

Practice with Tip: #21

Icing Consistency: Medium

Bag Position: 45° at 6:00

Hold Tip: Slightly Above Surface

The most popular icing technique of all, the shell is the basis for many borders. Lift the tip only slightly when piping shells to avoid a bumpy look.

1. Hold the bag in the 6:00 position so that you can pull the bag toward you. The tip should be slightly above the surface.

2. Squeeze hard, letting the icing fan out generously as it lifts the tip—do not lift the bag. Gradually relax your pressure as you lower the tip until it touches the surface.

3. Stop pressure and pull the tip away, without lifting it off the surface, to draw the shell to a point.

4. To make a shell border, start the end of your next shell so that the fanned end covers the tail of the preceding shell to form an even chain.

Bead

Practice with Tip: #5

Icing Consistency: Medium

Bag Position: 45° at 3:00 (9:00)

Hold Tip: Slightly Above Surface

If you can pipe a shell, you can pipe a bead—the movements are similar. To pipe a bead heart, simply pipe one bead, then a second, joining the tails. Smooth together using a decorator's brush.

1. Squeeze and lift the tip slightly so that icing fans out.

2. Relax pressure as you draw the tip down and bring the bead to a point.

3. To make a bead border, start the end of your next bead so that the fanned end covers the tail of the preceding bead to form an even chain.

Crown Border

Practice Tip: #32 for Shell, #4 for Dot

Icing Consistency: Medium

Bag Position: Slightly less than 90° at 6:00

Hold Tip: Slightly Above Surface

Majestic upright shells actually "crown" the top edges and sides of your cake. You can embellish the shell points with dots, stars or strings.

1. Start each shell just at the top edge of the cake; apply pressure to let the shell build up and curve over the edge of the tier.

2. Relax pressure and move down to draw the shell to a point. Continue piping a row of side-by-side shells over the top edge of your cake.

3. Pipe a tip 4 dot at the end of each shell. Optional: Use tip 3 to pipe double drop strings on shell ends, then pipe tip 4 dots at shell points.

FLEUR DE LIS FANTASY

Here is a quick-to-decorate cake done only in shells and the reverse shells of the fleur de lis. Fast but very impressive! Instructions on page 97.

Reverse Shell

Practice with Tip: #21

Icing Consistency: Medium

Bag Position: 45° at 6:00

Hold Tip: Slightly Above Surface

1. As you begin to form a shell, squeeze hard, letting the icing fan out.
2. Form a curve, moving the tip from 9:00 (3:00) to 12:00 to 6:00. Relax pressure and lower the tip, pulling straight toward you at 6:00 to form a tail.
3. Repeat with another shell, curving from 3:00 (9:00) to 12:00 to 6:00.
4. To make a reverse shell border, pipe a chain of swirling reverse shells, with the fan end of each new shell covering the tail of the previous shell. If you are making the border on a round cake, turn the cake as you go so that the back of the bag is at 6:00 and you are working toward yourself.

Opposite-facing shells look spectacular as top and bottom borders and as framed areas on your cake—they add a wonderful motion effect. The look is even fancier finished with a dot or a star at the center of each shell curve.

Fleur de Lis

Practice with Tip: #21

Icing Consistency: Medium

Bag Position: 45° at 6:00

Hold Tip: Slightly Above Surface

1. Pipe a basic shell, elongate the tail.
2. Keeping the bag at a 45° angle, pipe a reverse shell to the left of the center shell and join the tails.
3. Repeat procedure to the right side of the center shell.

Formerly a symbol of the royal coat of arms of France, this impressive decoration is now generally synonymous with anything French.

The swirled shells represent a lily.

Rope

Practice with Tip: #21

Icing Consistency: Medium

Bag Position: 45° at 4:30 (7:30)

Hold Tip: Lightly Touching Surface

A wonderful technique for finishing your piped baskets with pretty edging and handles. Excellent too for western or nautical theme cakes. You can make a great-looking rope with star or round tips (or basketweave tips, ridged or smooth side up).

1. Using a steady, even pressure, move the tip in a gentle sideways "S" curve. Stop pressure and pull tip away.
2. Insert tip under the bottom curve of the "S" shape.
3. Squeeze the bag with steady pressure as you pull down, then lift the tip. Move up and over the tail of the "S" as you continue to squeeze and form a hook.
4. Keep spacing as even as possible and "S" curves uniform in thickness, length and overall size. Be sure to tuck the tip into the bottom curve of the previous "S" before you begin squeezing, to insure the clean, continuous look of a rope.

Rosette

Practice with Tip: #16

Icing Consistency: Medium

Bag Position: 90°

Hold Tip: Slightly Above Surface

You can use rosettes in place of piped roses on the side of your cake—for the effect of a rose without the work. Rosettes are ideal candleholders, too; just pipe and position your candle in the center. They also look great finished with a center star or dot.

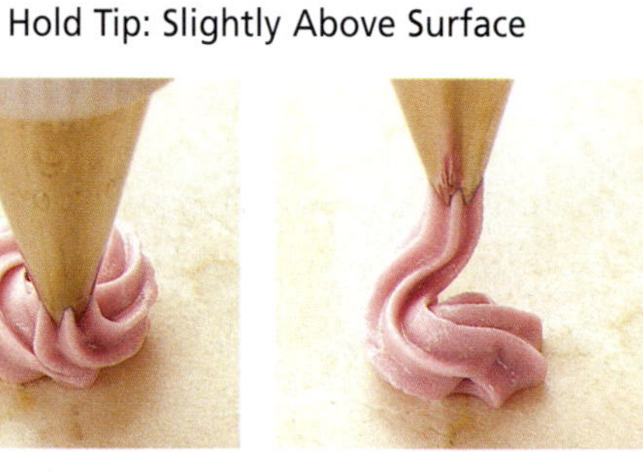

1. Keeping the tip slightly above surface, squeeze out icing to form a star and, without releasing pressure, move the tip in a tight complete rotation, starting at 9:00 (3:00), moving to 12:00...
2. then to 3:00 (9:00) and 6:00...
3. ...and ending back at 9:00 (3:00).
4. Stop pressure and lift tip away.

E-Motion

Practice with Tip: #16

Icing Consistency: Medium

Bag Position: 45° at 3:00 (9:00)

Hold Tip: Slightly Above Surface

These continuous e-shaped loops work best on a bottom border, or as a western lariat. If you have to stop on your border to change positions, push in your tip at the end of the "e" and continue piping to keep a smooth look.

1. Starting with bag at a 45° angle, and at bottom edge, squeeze out icing with even pressure, moving tip up to the right*...
2. ...and around as if writing the letter "e".
3. Repeat to complete the border, using a steady, even pressure.

To end, stop pressure, pull tip away. You can vary the look of the "e" motion border by making tight e's or stretched e's.

Lefties will pipe e's and c's by starting at the bottom edge, squeezing and moving up to left and around.

YEARS TO CHERISH

The exquisite heart cake is embellished with a flourish of rosettes and drop flowers. A subtle e-motion heart frames the message beautifully. Instructions on page 97.

SCROLL ENCHANTMENT

Perfectly spaced horizontal "c" scrolls draw the eye to the pretty petunias surrounding and crowning this cake. A wonderful springtime look. Instructions on page 98.

C-Motion

Practice with Tip: #16

Icing Consistency: Medium

Bag Position 45° at 3:00 (9:00)

Hold Tip: Slightly Above Surface

1. Squeezing out icing with even pressure, curve tip down and around to the right* as if writing a "c".

2. Repeat to complete the border, using a steady, even pressure.

3. To end, stop pressure, pull tip away.

Make waves using this fun technique. Stripe your decorating bag with piping gel for extra shimmer.

**Lefties will pipe e's and c's by starting at the bottom edge, squeezing and moving up to left and around.*

Horizontal "C"

Practice with Tip: #16

Icing Consistency: Medium

Bag Position: 90°

Hold Tip: Slightly Above Surface

1. Make a horizontal C-motion shell, relaxing pressure to taper the tail.

2. Make a reverse C-motion shell, but before piping the tail...

3. Relax pressure and taper tail to overlap the first C-motion shell tail.

Use a star or round tip to pipe this design on cake sides and tops. Blend the tails together and enhance with drop flowers for a professional look.

Pattern Press

Practice with Tip: #16

Icing Consistency: Medium

Bag Position: 45° at 3:00

Hold Tip: Slightly Above Surface

1. Lightly press pattern onto your iced cake to imprint the design.

2. Outline the imprinted design with icing, using the tip of your choice. Change the tip to change the look of each pattern.

The trick to uniform designs and steady writing and printing is using a pattern press! Simply imprint the press in all types of icing, including fondant! Use the vine pattern press on cake sides for a beautiful botanical effect.

Zigzag

Practice with Tip: #16

Icing Consistency: Medium

Bag Position: 45° at 3:00 (9:00)

Hold Tip: Lightly Touching Surface

1. Steadily squeeze and move your hand in a tight up and down motion.
2. Continue piping up and down with steady pressure. To end, stop pressure and pull tip away. For more elongated zigzags, move your hand to the desired height while maintaining a steady pressure. For a more relaxed look, just increase the width as you move the bag along.
3. Repeat as you move in a straight line with consistent up/down motion.

Popular way to fill in outlined areas, perfect for ribbed sweater and cuff effects. You can also use tight zigzags to cover the entire side of your cake—they look great!

Zigzag Puff

Practice with Tip: #17

Icing Consistency: Medium

Bag Position: 45° at 3:00 (9:00)

Hold Tip: Lightly Touching Surface

1. Begin to pipe with a light pressure, then use heavier pressure toward the center of the puff, then return gradually to a light pressure to form the tapered end.
2. To end each puff, stop pressure and pull tip away.
3. Repeat as you move in a straight line to form a row of puffs.

This is the fluffy look you want for making clouds and smoke. You'll also use zigzag puffs to add dimension as a side border.

Zigzag Garland

Practice with Tip: #16

Icing Consistency: Medium

Bag Position: 45° at 3:00 (9:00)

Hold Tip: Lightly Touching Surface

1. Mark cake for desired width and depth of garlands. Hold the bag as for basic zigzag technique. Touch the tip to first mark and squeeze with light, then heavy pressure in a tight up and down motion to form the curves of the garland as you pipe toward the center.
2. When you reach the center, reverse the process, piping heavy, then light toward the end.
3. To end, stop pressure and pull tip away. Practice for rhythmic pressure control—light/heavy/light—so garlands are uniform.

A beautiful beginning for a wedding cake border, ready to accompany with stringwork and flowers. Use a garland marker before piping to ensure evenly draping garlands.

Ruffle

Practice with Tip: #104

Icing Consistency: Medium

Bag Position: 45° at 3:00 (9:00)

Hold Tip: Wide End Lightly Touching Surface With Narrow End Facing Down And Away From Surface

Everyone loves a ruffle's graceful motion—ruffles always add interest to your cake. Use them as a top border, to frame a plaque or to trim doll dresses and baby bonnets.

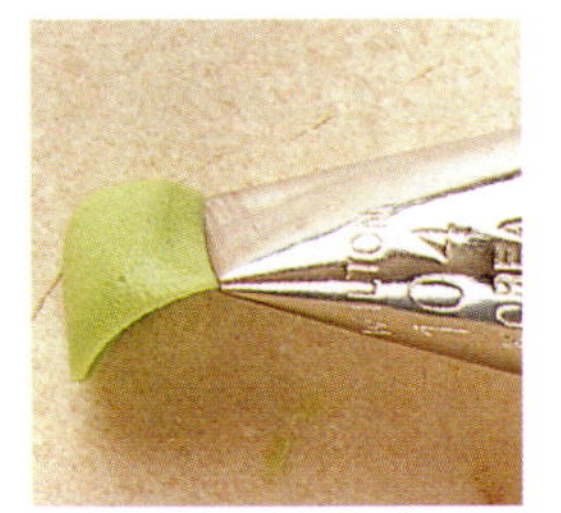

1. Keep the wide end of your tip always touching the cake, the narrow end down. Move wrist up to pull up icing.
2. Move wrist down to complete one curl of the ruffle.
3. Repeat up and down motion.
4. Raise and lower the narrow end as you move around the cake. Repeat this motion for the entire ruffle.

Ruffle Garland

Practice with Tip: #104

Icing Consistency: Medium

Bag Position: 45° at 4:30 (7:30)

Hold Tip: Wide End of Tip Touching Surface, Narrow End Facing Down And Away From Surface.

When ruffles drape over the sides of a wedding cake, the effect is of lighter-than-air elegance. Use also for bottom borders and doll dresses.

1. Mark the cake for the desired width and depth of garlands. Hold bag with tip positioned as for ruffles, but angle the narrow end about 1/4 inch away from surface. As you squeeze, move your hand up and down slightly to ruffle the icing.
2. Continue moving hand up and down as you position the bag to form the curve of the garland.
3. For a stand-up ruffle, just turn the tip so the narrow end is angled up and away from the surface and wide end is on surface.

THE BRIDE'S ENTRANCE

Her dress is a lovely swirl of ruffles, detailed with delicate sotas and dot lace. What an entrance! Instructions on page 98.

Swag

Practice with Tip: #104

Icing Consistency: Medium

Bag Position: 45° at 4:30 (7:30)

Hold Tip: Wide End Lightly Touching Surface, Narrow End Facing Down And Away From Surface

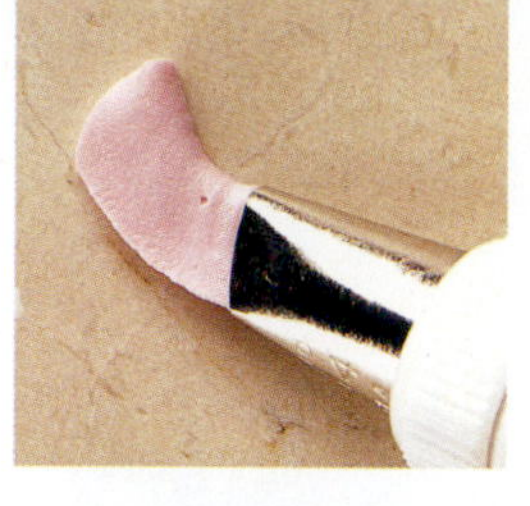

1. Use the same procedure as for the ruffle (p. 35), but keep bag straight without moving it up and down.

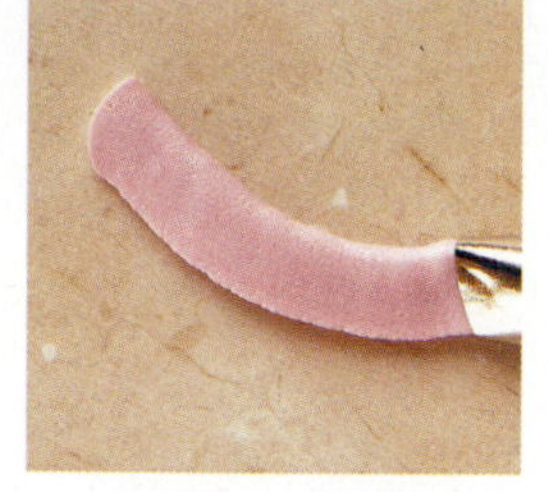

2. Keep pressure even as you form the curve.

3. Move up to end the swag. Repeat to create your continuous swag border.

A charming addition to cake sides, the swag can also be used in non-traditional designs. Try framing the cake's top edge with a swag. Overpipe for an interesting effect. Pipe a swag as a banner across the cake, adding a tip #1 message.

Bow

Practice with Tip: #104

Icing Consistency: Medium

Bag Position: 45° at 6:00

Hold Tip: Wide End Touching Surface, Narrow End Straight Up

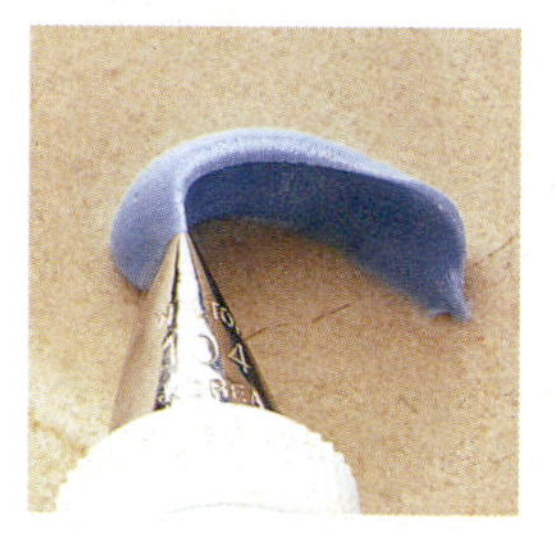

1. With narrow end of tip pointing straight up, squeeze, moving the tip up and around to the left and back to the starting point.

2. Continue around, making a second loop on the right.

3. The two loops will form a figure 8.

4. While holding bag in the same position, return to the center and squeeze out two streamers.

From tiny shoestrings on figure piped booties to an enormous ribbon covering an entire cake top, the bow has many uses. Create a different look each time you use a different tip: round, star or petal.

Flute

Practice with Tip: #21 for Shell, #104 for Flute

Icing Consistency: Medium

Bag Position: 30° at 6:00

Hold Tip: Touching Between Shells

1. Enhance your shell borders with this pretty effect. Hold the bag so that the wide end of the tip is between two shells.

2. Squeeze and move tip up slightly as icing fills in between shells.

3. Stop pressure, lower tip, and pull away.

Decorators love this elegant embellishment to a row of shells, because it's so simple to do! Adding a bit more spacing between the shells will prevent the flutes from crushing the shells' delicate ridges.

GARDEN GARLANDS

Majestic triple swag garlands set the stage for your brightly colored fresh flowers. Instructions on page 98.

Drop String

Practice with Tip: #3

Icing Consistency: Stiff Icing, Thinned With Corn Syrup

Bag Position: Shoulder Level at 4:30 (7:30)

Hold Tip: Lightly Touching Surface To Attach

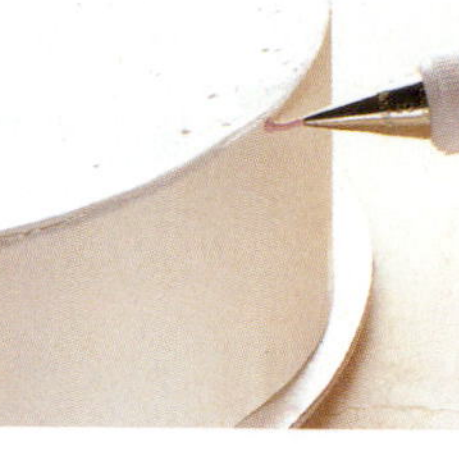

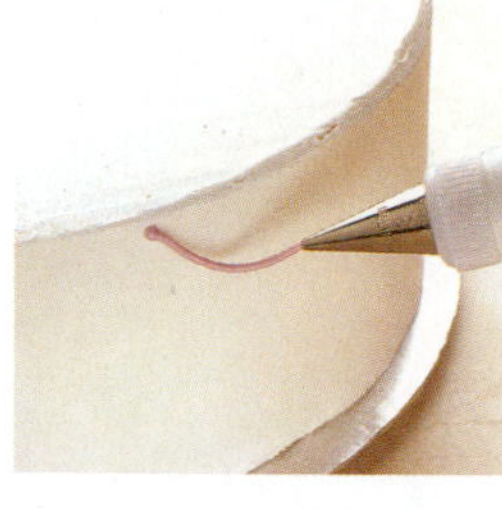

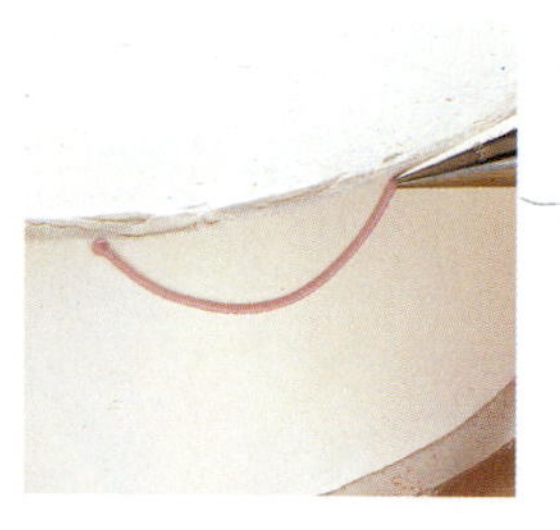

1. With a toothpick, mark horizontal divisions on cake in the width you desire. Touch tip to first mark and squeeze, pausing momentarily so that icing sticks to surface.
2. While squeezing, pull the bag toward you. Continue squeezing to allow the icing to drape naturally into an arc. Icing will drop by itself—do not move the tip down with the string. The end of the tip should be the same distance from the surface as the width from point to point on your cake.
3. Stop pressure before you touch tip to second mark to end string. Repeat, keeping drop strings uniform in length and width.

The trick to these flowing strings is to pull the bag toward you as the string drapes down. If you "draw" the string with the tip, you won't achieve a pretty curve and your strings will tend to break. Pipe at eye level to your cake so that strings line up evenly. The Wilton Cake Divider Set is a great help in accurately dividing and marking your cake for even drop strings.

Double Drop String

Practice with Tip: #3

Icing Consistency: Stiff Icing Slightly Thinned With Corn Syrup

Bag Position: Shoulder Level at 4:30 (7:30)

Hold Tip: Lightly Touching Surface To Attach

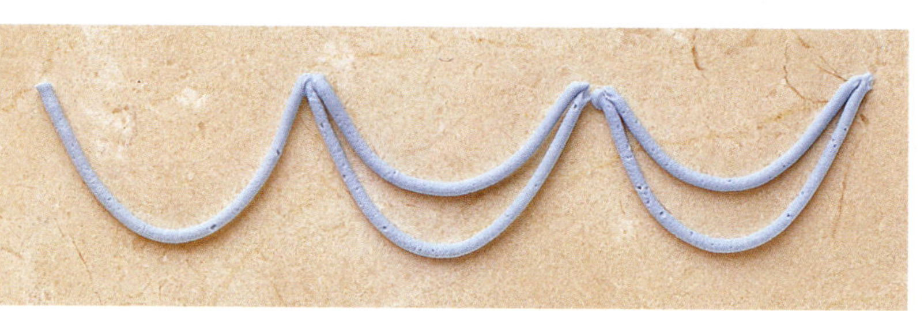

1. Mark cake for your longest row of drop strings, then pipe that row.
2. Return to the first drop string point, squeeze the bag, and drop a string with a slightly shorter arc than in the first row. Join end of this string to the end of the corresponding string in the first row.

For all multiple drop strings, it's fun to use multiple colors, too. Put favorite holiday colors together to really dress up your cake for the occasion.

SWEPT UP IN ROMANCE

Often the simplest wedding designs work best. Gentle drop strings and zigzag garlands carry the day. Instructions on page 96.

Triple Drop String

Practice with Tip: #3

Icing Consistency: Stiff Icing, Slightly Thinned With Corn Syrup

Bag Position: Shoulder Level at 4:30 (7:30)

Hold Tip: Lightly Touching Surface To Attach

1. Mark cake for your longest row of drop strings, then pipe that row.
2. Pipe a shorter middle row, joining the ends of each string to the ends of the corresponding first row strings.
3. Pipe the third row: Return to the drop string point, squeeze the bag, and drop a string with a slightly shorter arc than in the second row. Join the end of this string to the ends of the corresponding first and second row strings.

Your practice board can really help you to make perfect drop strings. Just set it upright, at eye level, and practice keeping your strings evenly spaced and aligned. Pretty soon, you'll be piping multiple strings with ease.

Overlapping Triple Drop String

Practice with Tip: #3

Icing Consistency: Stiff Icing, Slightly Thinned With Corn Syrup

Bag Position: Shoulder Level at 4:30 (7:30)

Hold Tip: Lightly Touching Surface To Attach

1. Pipe one group of triple drop strings, longest string first, middle string second and shortest string last.
2. Pipe a second trio of triple drop strings, starting midway between the first set.
3. Repeat groups of drop strings to form a beautiful overlapping border.

These interlocking groups of strings look intricate; but once you know the tricks of piping drop strings, they are no problem. Try piping each set of 3 in a different color.

Garland & String

Practice with Tips: #16, 3

Icing Consistency: Medium

Bag Position: 45° at 4:30 (7:30)

Hold Tip: Lightly Touching Surface

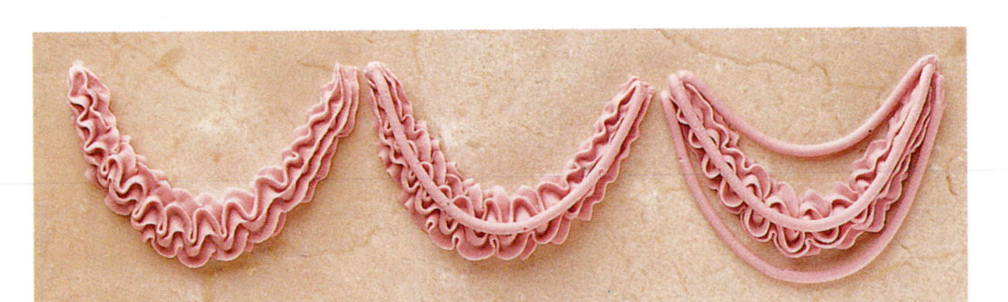

1. Mark cake for garland. Use tip 16. Hold bag as for basic zigzag procedure (p. 34). Use light-to-heavy-to-light pressure to form curves of garland between marks. To end, stop pressure, pull tip away.
2. Use tip 3. Touch tip to first garland point and pipe a single drop string, positioning on center of garland. Attach to next garland point.
3. Drop single strings as in step 2, positioning above and below garland. Continue to cover entire garland.

To enhance your zigzag garlands, overpipe with one to three drop strings. You can also highlight the garland points with dots, stars or drop flowers.

Printing

Practice with Tip: #3 with message press

Icing Consistency: Thin

Bag Position: 45° at 3:00

Hold Tip: Slightly Touching Surface

You may pipe letters freehand, pipe over a pattern traced with a toothpick, or pipe after imprinting letters with a pattern press. If you are using a pattern press, let icing crust slightly, then imprint the message. With a steady, even pressure, squeeze out a straight line, lifting the tip off the surface to let icing string drop. To prevent tails from forming, be careful to stop squeezing before you touch tip to surface and pull away. Be sure the end of the tip is clean before you go on to another line.

Fancy Printing

Practice with Tip: #2 with message press

Practice with Tip: #14 bouncing letters

Practice with Tip: #45 flat lettering

Practice with Tip: #3 balls

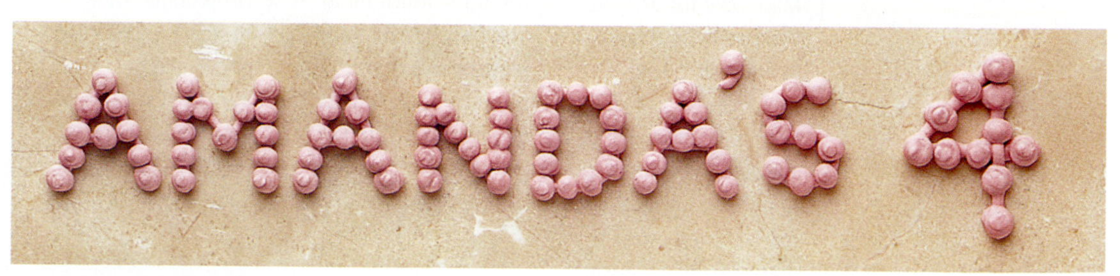

Practice with Tip: #5

Icing Consistency: Thin

Bag Position: 45° angle at 3:00

Hold Tip: Slightly Touching Surface

You may pipe letters freehand, pipe over a pattern traced with a toothpick, or pipe after imprinting letters with a pattern press. If you are using a pattern press, let icing crust slightly, then imprint the message. Steadily squeeze, gliding along the surface in a smooth, continuous motion. Remember to keep your wrist straight, moving your entire forearm in a single unit. Use your arm, not your fingers, to form each line, letter or word. After you begin to master the curves and swings of the letters, lift the tip up slightly as you write. You'll find you have more control if you let the icing draw out slightly over the surface as you write.

Fancy Writing

Practice with Tip: #101s calligraphy

Practice with Tip: #3

Practice with Tip: #2 with message press

Practice with Tip: #1 with message press

Figure Piping

Whether you are piping clowns, wild animals or members of the family, figure piping is one way you can really add some personality to your cake. Your figures can be as lifelike or cartoonish as you want them to be. Begin with a base, then add familiar shapes such as dots, balls and strings that give the figure personality. Once you have mastered pressure control, figure piping will be easy.

Stiff consistency icing is the key element to successful figure piping. For softer figures that are more fun to eat, use buttercream icing. With buttercream, you can pipe figures directly on your cake, shortly ahead of the party. Royal icing shapes dry very hard, so they can be difficult to eat, but you can make them well in advance of the party. Pipe them ahead of time on waxed paper, let dry, then position figures on cake. Remember to store pre-made royal icing decorations in a cool, dry and dark place. Exposure to bright sunlight or constant fluorescent lighting can cause colors to fade.

Upright

Hold tip at 90° angle with the end of the tip slightly above surface. Start squeezing, applying a steady, even pressure. As the icing begins to build up, raise the tip with it, but keep its end buried in the icing. To complete your shape, stop squeezing as you bring the end of the tip to the surface.

Horizontal

Hold tip at 45° angle and lightly touch tip to surface. Apply pressure as you move the tip to let the shape build. It's essential that the tip remains buried in the icing as it is squeezed out. Stop squeezing as you bring the end of the tip to the surface.

Additional Piping

Once you've piped the basic body or bottom portion of you figure, you can add other elements directly onto that basic shape. Tuck the tip into the basic figure, apply pressure and move tip to create the shape you need. Stop squeezing and pull tip away. In this way, you can add heads, arms, legs, fruit stems, etc.

Animals Sitting

Basic Upright Torsos
Use a large round tip for torso—12, 1A, or 2A. Use heavy pressure, gradually relaxing as you move up. Stop pressure completely and pull away.

Adding Limbs
Use tip 10 to pull out arms and 12 for legs. Add head and features for the animal you are piping.

Teddy Bear
Use Brown and Black Icing Colors.
Pipe tip 1A body and 2A head, tip 5 muzzle, tip 12 legs, tip 10 arms, tip 2 dot and string facial features, tip 2 ears.

Chick
Use Lemon Yellow and Golden Yellow combined, Orange and Black Icing Colors.
Pipe tip 2A body and head, tip 2 dot eyes and cheeks, tip 2 pull-out dot beak and feet, tip 349 top feathers, tip 67 wings.

Elephant
Use Pink and Black Icing Colors.
Pipe tip 1A body, tip 2A head, tip 12 legs and trunk, tip 104 ears, tip 1 dot eyes, pull- out dot tusks and string features.

Penguin
Use Black and Orange Icing Colors.
Pipe tip 12 body and head, tip 3 stomach, facemask and feet, tip 1 dot eyes and pull-out dot beak, tip 6 arms.

Animals Lying

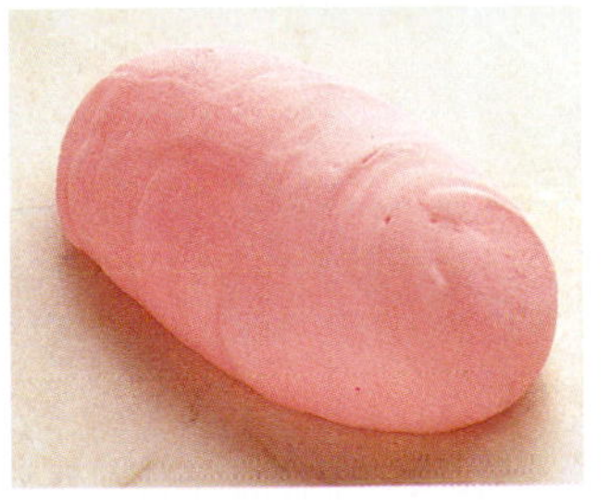

Body
Use a large round tip for body—12, 1A, or 2A. Use heavy pressure, gradually relaxing as you move up. Stop pressure completely and pull away.

Head
Use a large round tip for head, same size as for body or smaller. Place tip at top of body and pipe a smaller, round ball.

Pig
Use Pink and Black Icing Colors.
Pipe tip 2A body, tip 12 head, tip 6 snout, tip 8 legs, tip 2 dot eyes and curly string tail, tip 81 ears.

Lamb
Use Black and Pink Icing Colors.
Pipe tip 2A body, tip 12 head, tip 13 zigzag fur, tip 5 legs and muzzle, tip 81 ears, tip 3 hooves, tip 1 dot facial features.

Cat
Use Lemon Yellow and Black Icing Colors.
Pipe tip 1A body, tip 12 head, tip 8 legs, tip 3 ears and cheeks, tip 1 dot and string facial features.

Dog
Use Brown and Black Icing Colors.
Pipe tip 2A body, tip 12 head, tip 5 muzzle, tip 6 legs, tip 4 ears with tip 1 fur, tip 1 pull-out dot fur, tip 4 tail, tip 1 dot and string facial features.

Seal
Use Black Icing Color.
Pipe tip 2A elongated body, tip 12 head, tip 8 flippers and tail, tip 1 dot and string facial features.

Turtle
Use Moss Green, Brown and Black Icing Colors.
Pipe tip 1A body, tip 10 elongated ball head, tip 10 ball legs, tip 5 dot spots (flatten), tip 2 pull-out dot tail, tip 1 dot eyes and string mouth.

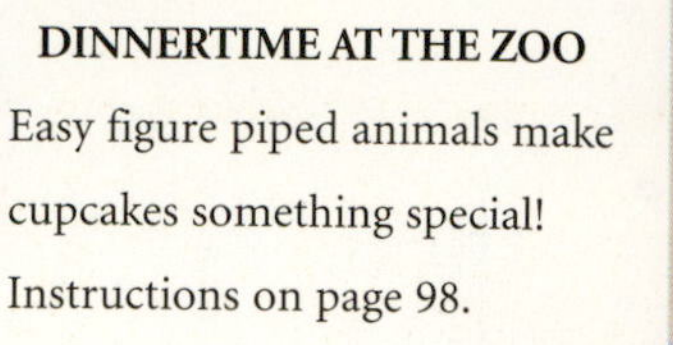
DINNERTIME AT THE ZOO

Easy figure piped animals make cupcakes something special! Instructions on page 98.

Apple & Cherry

Use Christmas Red, Brown and Leaf Green Icing Colors.
Apple: Pipe tip 6 ball, tip 2 string stem, tip 349 leaf.
Cherry: Pipe tip 3 dot, tip 2 string stem, tip 349 leaf.

Pear

Use Leaf Green and Brown Icing Colors. Pipe tip 6 ball, decrease pressure and elongate shape. Add tip 2 pull-out dot stem.

Banana

Use Golden Yellow and Brown Icing Colors. Pipe tip 5 string using heavy pressure, stop pressure and remove tip. Add tip 2 dots at each end for stems.

Grapes

Use Violet, Brown and Leaf Green Icing Colors. Pipe tip 3 dots, add tip 3 string stem and tip 349 leaf.

Other Fruit

Use the following techniques to create your favorite fruit. Want pumpkins?—Use Orange Icing Color, pipe tip 7 pumpkin shape and add tip 4 Brown stem. Pineapples?—Combine Golden Yellow with a small amount of Brown and pipe tip 7 pineapple shape, cover with tip 16 stars; add tip 352 pull-out leaf Kelly Green stalks. Peaches?—Combine Creamy Peach with Orange and pipe tip 6 peach shape, add tip 2 Brown pull-out dot stem and tip 66 Leaf Green leaf.

Balloon

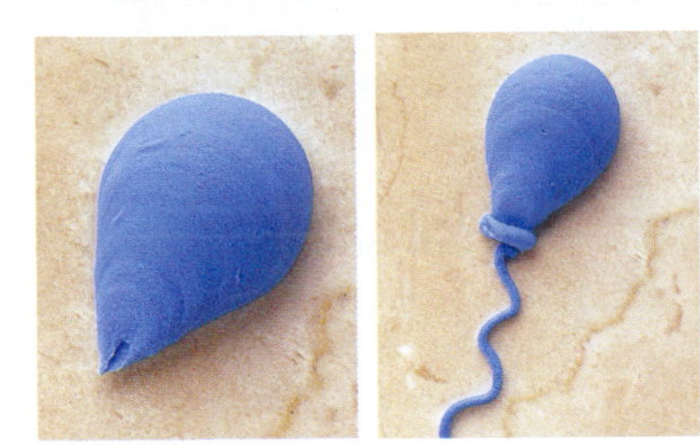

Use Royal Blue Icing Color. Pipe tip 12 bead (see page 28). Apply heavy pressure, pull back tip slightly and decrease pressure, bringing end to a point. Stop pressure and pull tip away. Add tip 2 neck and string.

Faces

Use Copper (Lt. Skintone) and Brown Icing Colors. Faces begin with tip 12 ball shapes; we've added features in the following colors: Lemon Yellow, Black, Christmas Red, Royal Blue, Copper. Choose your colors to match people you know!

Male—tip 3 dot eyes, nose and ears, tip 1 string mouth, tip 1 curly string hair.

Female—tip 2 dot eyes and nose, tip 1 string mouth, tip 1 curly string hair.

Baby with bonnet—tip 101s ruffle bonnet, tip 2 dot eyes, ears and nose, tip 1 string mouth, tip 1 dot pacifier.

Heart

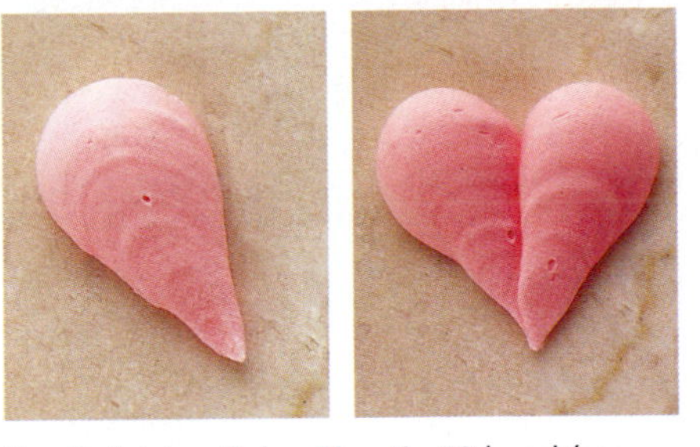

Use Pink Icing Color. Pipe tip 12 bead (see page 28). Apply heavy pressure, move tip slightly and decrease pressure, bringing end to a point. Repeat to pipe a second shape, gradually decreasing pressure and joining tail of first, forming a "V" shape.

FANCY FRUITCAKE

A great party pick—you can pipe the royal icing fruit in advance, then add stems and leaves before serving.

Instructions on page 99.

Basketweave

Practice with Tip: #47

Icing Consistency: Medium

Bag Position: 45° at 6:00 for Vertical Stripes; at 3:00 (9:00) for Horizontal Bars

Hold Tip: Lightly Touching Surface, Serrated Side Up

1. Squeeze out a vertical stripe of icing from top to bottom.
2. Squeeze out short horizontal stripes of icing across the vertical stripe starting at the top. Spacing between stripes should be the same as the width of the tip opening. Squeeze next vertical stripe over ends of horizontal stripes. Start next set of horizontal stripes by burying the tip under the first vertical stripe.
3. Repeat vertical lines then horizontal lines until you achieve basketweave effect. Each new set should fit between the previous set.

This wonderful technique turns any size cake or cupcakes into beautiful baskets. Try using different tips to vary the woven effects. Imagine a floral Easter, Mother's Day, bridal or summertime theme cake covered in basketweave—spectacular!

Basketweave Variations

Practice with Tips: Combine #47 and Tip 16

Practice with Tip: #44

Practice with Tip: #17 Star Tip

Practice with Tips: Combine #7 and #47

SPRING FLOWER BASKET

Royal icing daisies and drop flowers in two sizes create a lavish top border on this unforgettable heart cake. The intricate basketweave effect and rope bottom border add outstanding texture. Instructions on page 96.

BABY BEAR

Character cakes covered with stars are probably the most requested designs. Here's a great example, highlighted by a ruffle bib and puff bottom border. Instructions on page 99.

Outline

Practice with Tip: #3

Icing Consistency: Thin

Bag Position: 45° at 3:00 (9:00)

Hold Tip: Slightly Above Surface

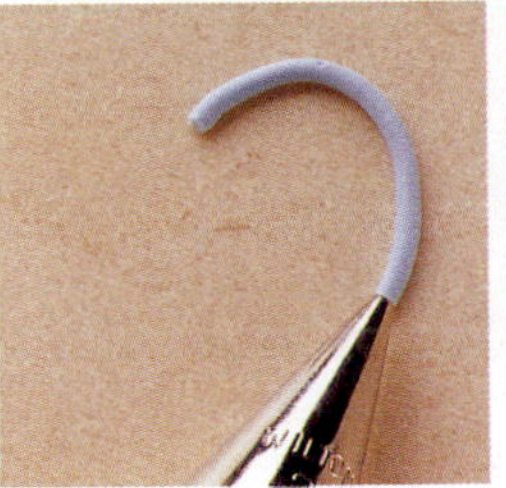

1. Touch tip to surface. Raise the tip slightly and continue to squeeze.

2. The icing will flow out of the tip while you direct it along the surface.

3. To end, stop squeezing, touch tip to surface and pull away.

One of the essential techniques for a character cake. Characters or designs are often outlined first, then piped in with stars or zigzags. Outline facial features, too. Color flow plaques are also outlined before icing is flowed into the shape.

Star Fill In

Practice with Tip: #16

Icing Consistency: Medium

Bag Position: 90°, Straight Up

Hold Tip: ¼ Inch Above Surface

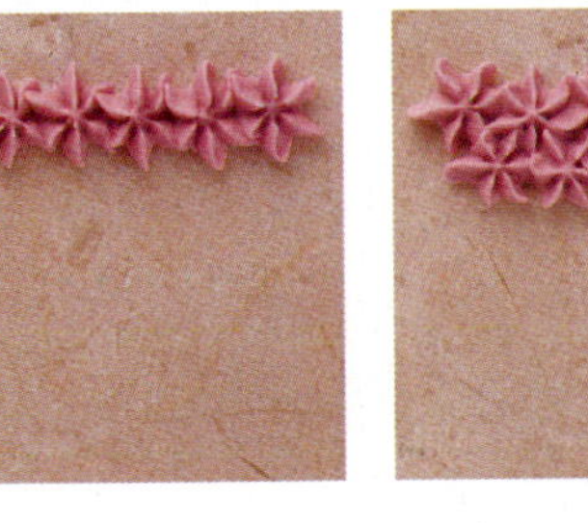

1. Pipe a row of stars evenly and close together, adjusting the tip position slightly each time so that the points of the stars interlock and cover the area without any gaps.

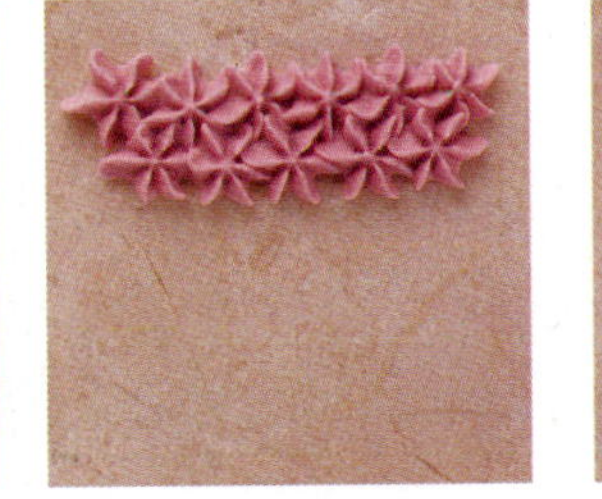

2. Pipe a row of stars beneath the first, again adjusting tip position to close any gaps.

3. Continue to fill in entire area.

Because these close-together stars require so much piping from the same bag, it's a good idea to keep replenishing the icing. Change your icing when soft or stars will be poorly defined.

Triple Star

Practice with Tip: #2010

Use Large Coupler

Icing Consistency: Medium

Bag Position: 90°, Straight Up

Hold Tip: ¼ Inch Above Surface

1. Pipe one group of triple stars.

2. As you pipe more stars, turn tip slightly so that stars interlock and area is covered without any gaps.

3. Continue piping stars and turning tip to fill in entire area. If you need to fill in missed areas, use tip 18.

Tip 2010 pipes three perfect tip 18-sized stars at a time, making it fast and easy to fill in your cake. The proper wrist motion is essential to ensure that groups of stars interlock.

Lattice

Practice with Tip: #2

Icing Consistency: Stiff Icing Thinned with Corn Syrup

Bag Position: 45° at 4:30 (7:30)

Hold Tip: Slightly Above Surface

1. Outline the shape to be covered using tip 2.

2. Starting in the center of the outlined shape, pipe tip 2 diagonal strings to the right, attached to outline.

3. From the opposite side, pipe diagonal strings in the other direction, covering the area.

Reminiscent of garden themes, lattice can cover garland sections, imprinted areas, even entire sides of cake with spectacular results. Vary your tip selections for different looks—try round, star or basketweave tips.

Sotas

Practice with Tip: #1

Icing Consistency: Thin

Bag Position: 90°

Hold Tip: Slightly Above Surface

1. Squeeze bag and allow icing to drop randomly in a series of overlapping loops. Cover area edge-to-edge.

An impressive, yet quick and easy technique you can perfect on the first try! The lacy texture of sotas looks magnificent on borders, outlined areas, and as a background for flowers. The keys to simply executed sotas are thinned icing and using a small amount of icing in your bag—this puts less pressure on your hands.

Cornelli

Practice with Tip: #1 or 2

Icing Consistency: Thin

Bag Position: 90°

Hold Tip: Close To Cake So That Icing Attaches Without Scraping Cake With Tip And Without Flattening Icing Strings

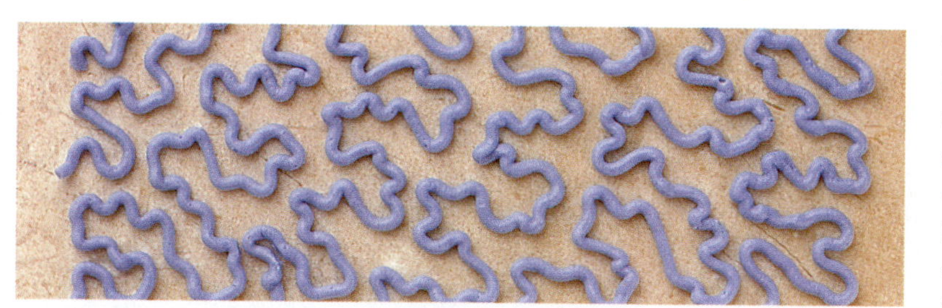

1. Beginning and ending at edges, pipe a continuous string of icing, curve it up, down and around until area is covered. Make certain strings never touch or cross. Don't leave any loose ends! Stop pressure; pull tip away.

Cornelli Lace is the perfect look for a formal presentation, such as wedding and anniversary cakes. The precise, lacy design of this freehand technique depends on continuous curving strings that do not overlap or touch.

Combing

Practice with Wilton Decorating Comb or Triangle

Icing Consistency: Medium-To-Thin Buttercream

Use the Wilton Decorating Comb or Decorating Triangle to add different contoured effects to your iced cake.

Choose the type of effect you want—wide or narrow—then run that edge around your cake side to form beautiful ridges.

Ridges will be deep or shallow depending on the side of decorating comb or triangle you use.

For an interesting cake decorating effect, try combing! It's a fast way to cover larger areas with texture. Cover the cake with a slightly thicker coating of icing so the comb's ridges do not touch the cake. Comb immediately after icing cake, while icing is soft. Using a turntable helps to keep the movement smooth.

Combed Garland

Practice with Wilton Decorating Comb

Icing Consistency: Medium-To-Thin Buttercream

To create a garland, hold comb so that about 4 teeth from the edge are touching the cake at the

beginning of garland. Run comb in a curve, positioning so that about 6 teeth are touching

cake at the bottom of the garland, then curve back with 4 teeth touching to finish garland.

Garlands sculpted with the decorating comb add texture and drama to any cake design, and are easy to do! It's important to keep the comb level with the cake surface, so that the ridges created are uniform. Try combining this technique with strings, fleur-de-lis or beads.

TOUCH OF CHOCOLATE

Achieve the look of a rich continental dessert with ease. Cake sides are neatly combed; simple rosettes and pull-out stars add dimension. Instructions on page 99.

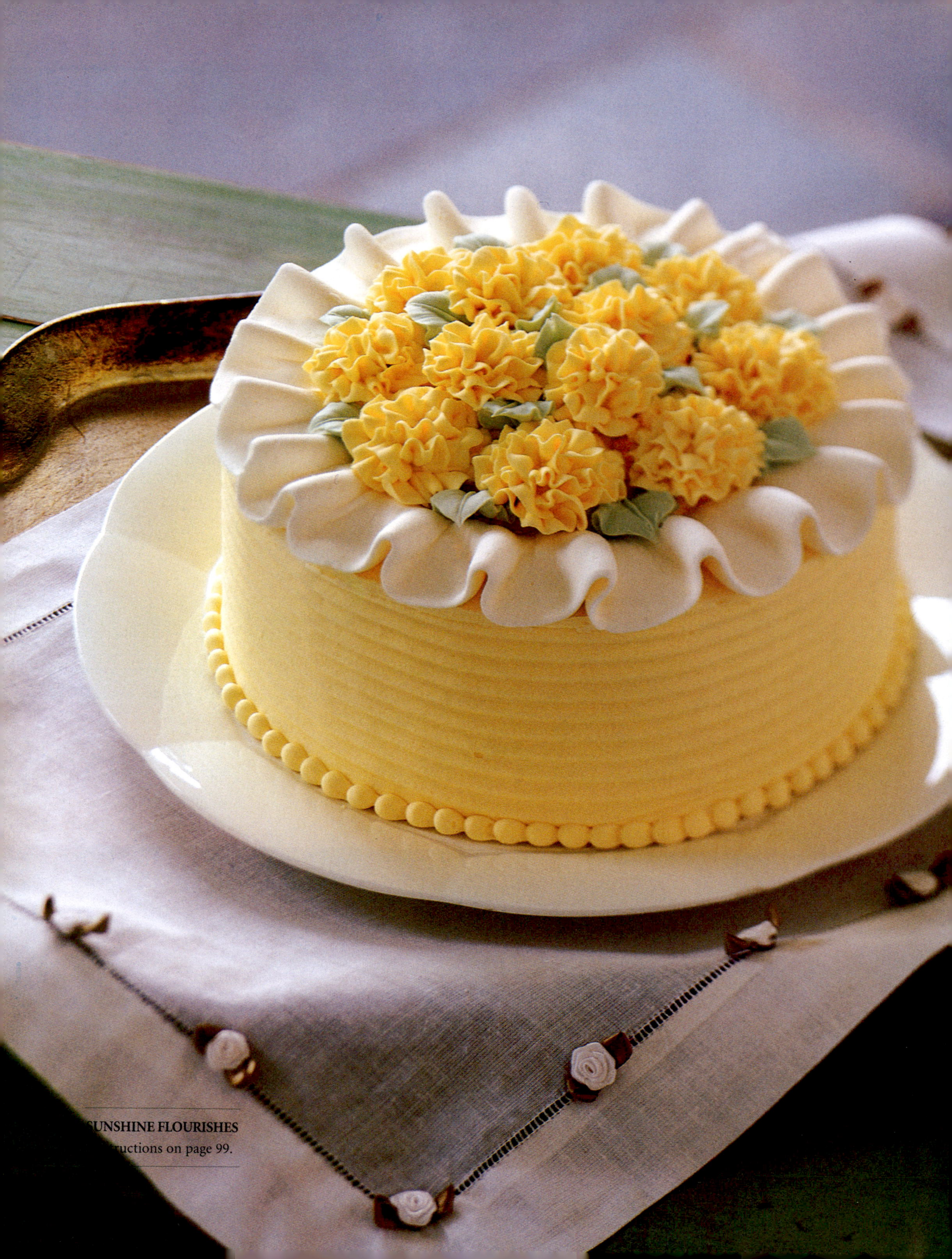

SUNSHINE FLOURISHES

ructions on page 99.

Flower Making

Alone or gathered in bunches, icing flowers make a cake blossom. Explore beautiful flowers like the sweet pea, carnation or forget-me-not, which add lovely color to your cake design. Create the magnificent rose—the most popular icing flower of all—then progress to the grandest bell-shaped lilies. With practice, your flowers will have the just-picked look of real garden flowers.

Rosebud

Practice with Tips: #104, 3

Icing Consistency: Buttercream—Stiff Consistency For Petals, Thin Consistency For Sepals And Calyx

Bag Position: 45° at 4:30 (7:30) For Petals, 45° at 6:00 For Sepals And Calyx

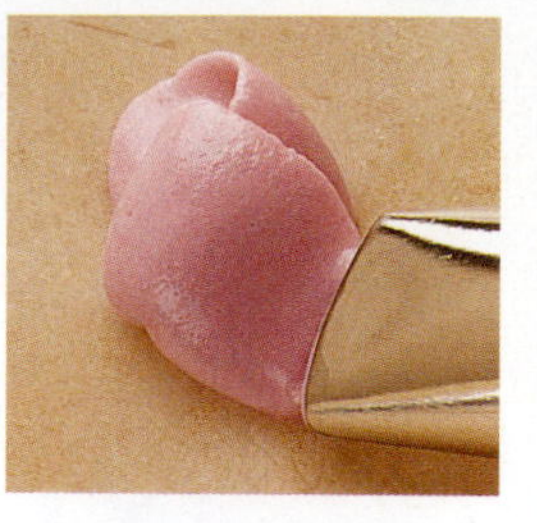

1. Using tip 104, make the base petal. Keep the narrow end of the tip raised up and slightly to the right (left for lefties). While squeezing, move the tip along the surface away from you in a straight line about 1/4 inch long. Pause, then continue squeezing as the icing fans out. Returning the tip to the original position and halfway back, start to release pressure, move tip to starting point, stop pressure and pull tip away.
2. Using tip 104, make the overlapping petal. Touch the wide end of the tip to the outside edge of completed petal. The bag is positioned as for the base petal, at 4:30 (7:30); hold it steady in this position until the second petal is completed. As you continue squeezing, the icing will catch the edge of the base petal and roll it over naturally. When the second petal looks complete, stop pressure completely, touch the tip back down to the surface and pull tip away.
3. Using tip 3, make the sepals and calyx. Form the middle sepal first by squeezing and letting icing build up. Lift the bag up and away from the flower. Stop pressure as you pull away to form the point of the sepal. Repeat, making a sepal on the left and right sides. For the calyx, insert tip into the base of the center sepal. Squeeze, letting the icing build up. Slowly draw the tip toward you, relaxing pressure as you move away from the flower. Stop pressure, pull away. You may want to blend the calyx into the stem using a dampened decorator brush.

Finish your petit fours or cupcakes with one pretty rosebud. Made in buttercream, this flat flower can be piped directly on the cake in your favorite colors.

Half Rose

Practice with Tips: #104, 3

Icing Consistency: Buttercream—Stiff For Petals, Thin For Calyx

Bag Position: For Right Petal, 45° at 7:30 (4:30); For Left Petal, 45° at 4:30 (7:30); For Sepals and Calyx, 45° at 6:00.

Hold Tip: Wide End of Tip Resting on Surface

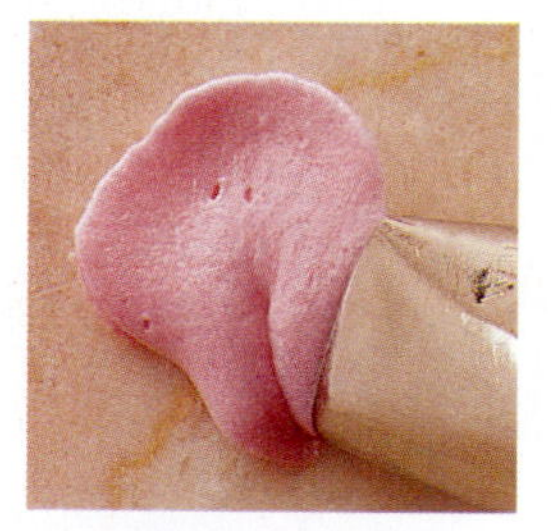

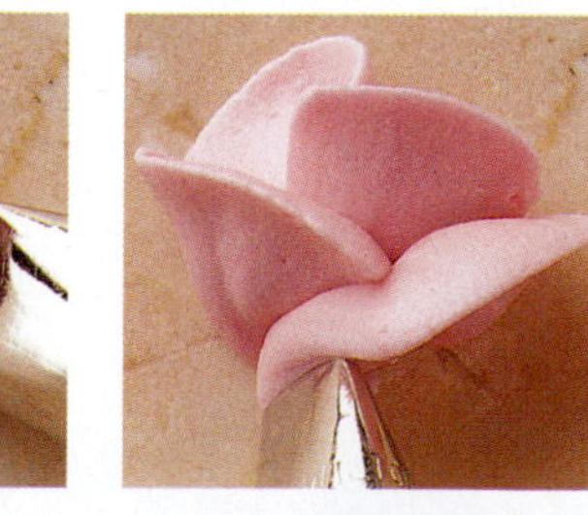

1. Make a rosebud without sepals and calyx. To make left petal: Hold the bag at a 45° angle so the end of bag points to the right (left for lefties); fingertips gripping the bag should face you. Touch wide end of tip 104 to the bottom left side of rosebud. Squeeze, move it up, around to the right and down, relaxing pressure.
2. To make right petal: Hold bag at a 45° angle so the end of bag points to the left (right for lefties). Touch wide end of tip to bottom right side of rosebud base. Squeeze, move up, around to the left and down to the center of bud base. Stop pressure and pull tip away.
3. Make sepals and calyx with tip 3 and thinned icing. Follow same procedure as for step 3 of rosebud, starting at bottom center of half rose.

The half rose is really a rosebud with two side petals. You can also give your half roses a fuller look by adding two or three more side petals.

Sweet Pea

Practice with Tips: #104, 3

Icing Consistency: Buttercream—Stiff for Petals, Thin for Calyx

Bag Position: For Center Petal And Calyx, 45° at 6:00; For Left Petal, 45° at 4:30; For Right Petal, 45° at 7:30.

Hold Tip: Wide End Touching Surface; Narrow End Straight Up

1. Make the center petal. Squeeze the bag and lift the tip slightly off the surface (about 1/4 inch) as the icing moves forward and curls. Continue to squeeze without changing position. Relax pressure, and return the tip to the surface. Stop squeezing, pull tip away.
2. Make the side petals. Position your bag slightly to the left of the center petal. Follow the same procedure as you did for the center petal—squeeze, and while the petal curls, lift the tip, relaxing your pressure and lowering the tip back to the surface. Stop squeezing and pull away. Repeat for the right side petal, holding the tip to the right of the center petal.
3. Make the calyx with tip 3.

Here is one of the fastest, easiest-to-make flowers in the garden. Sweet peas work beautifully as part of a floral cascade in corners of wedding or Mother's Day cakes. Try piping them in variegated shades.

PETIT FOURS

Little cakes make such a big impression. Everyone loves to be served these individually decorated desserts, which are covered in luscious poured fondant. Instructions on page 102.

Lily of the Valley

Practice with Tips: #70, 81, 2, 1

Icing Consistency: Buttercream—Medium

Bag Position: For Leaf And Stems, 45° at 3:00 (9:00), For Flowers, 30° Angle at 4:30 (7:30)

Hold Tip: Above Decorating Surface For Flowers, Slightly Touching Surface For Leaf And Stems

This demure shoot of delicate blossoms is a traditional choice for spring. To create a 3-D leaf effect, angle the top edge of the decorating tip to about 45°. The greater the angle, the more dimension your leaf will have.

1. Make the leaf: Using tip 70, squeeze out icing, letting it build up slightly for a broad width. Move upward, curve to right and gradually stop pressure to bring leaf to a point.
2. Make the stems: Add a tip 2 stem along the center of leaf, moving off to an angle. Pipe short secondary stems outward from the main stem.
3. Make the flowers: Using tip 81, squeeze with light pressure ABOVE the surface with the inner curve of tip facing you. Press out a curve of icing and continue squeezing until a tiny bell shape is formed. Stop pressure. Lightly touch the tip to surface; give one more quick squeeze, stop and lift away. Add two tip 1 stamens to center.

Half Carnation

Practice with Tips: #150, 3

Icing Consistency: Buttercream—Stiff

Bag Position: Center Petal, 45° at 6:00; Side Petals, 45°at 4:30 (left) and 7:30 (right)

Hold Tip: One End Touching Surface, Other End Straight Up

Achieve the beautiful ruffled effect of a full carnation, piped directly on your cake. Be sure to use stiff consistency icing to hold each petal's shape.

1. Make the center petal: With wide end touching the surface and narrow end straight up, start squeezing, moving tip straight up and down in a jiggling motion (similar to sweet pea technique but with narrower petals). Stop squeezing and pull away.
2. Make the side petals: With bag at 4:30, place the wide end of tip at the base of the first petal and squeeze out two left side petals using the same jiggle motion. For two right side petals, place bag at 7:30 and squeeze in the same fashion, to form a fan-shaped row of petals.

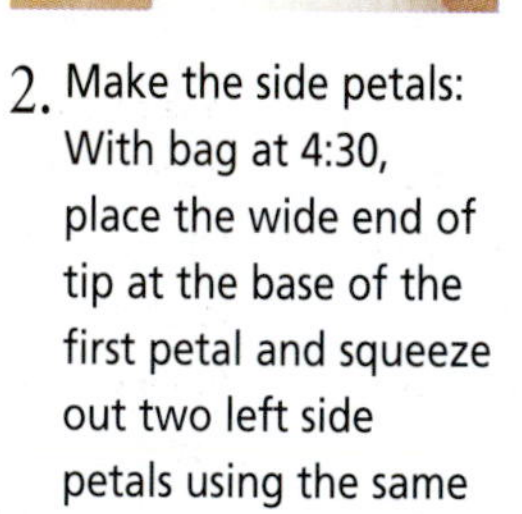

3. With bag at 4:30 and 7:30, pipe a ruffled petal between each petal. Add tip 3 sepals.

SWANS AFLOAT

A serene swan duo drifts among lush lilies of the valley and a pretty leaf border. Instructions on page 100.

Royal Icing Flowers on Wires

Practice with Tips: #4, 3, 352
Icing Consistency: Stiff Royal Icing

Bag Position: 90° Straight Up
Hold Tip: Lightly Touching Surface

Be sure the floral wire you are using is wrapped with floral tape. **Wire or floral tape should never be inserted directly into a cake**—use flower spikes to hold wired flowers.

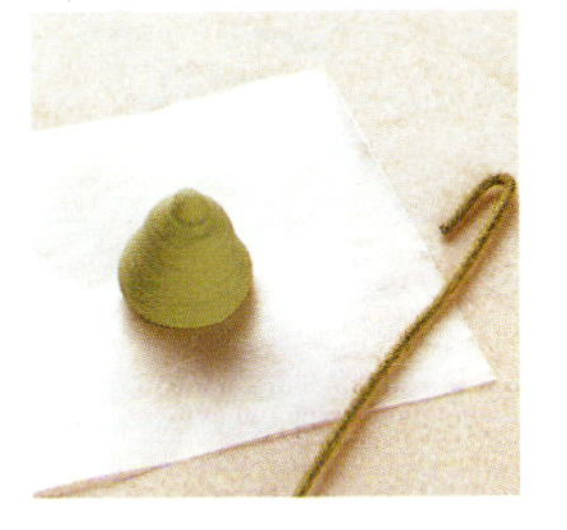

1. On waxed paper square, using royal icing, pipe a tip 4 dot base. Make 1/8 inch hook on one end of 4 inch cloth-covered florist wire or craft wire which has been wrapped with florist tape.
2. Insert hook into base. With slightly moistened decorator brush, smooth and taper icing on the wire.
3. Push other end of wire into a piece of styrofoam to dry base.
4. Remove waxed paper and attach flower with dots of icing. For leaves, Pipe tip 3 royal icing dot on a waxed paper square and immediately lay hooked end of wrapped wire in dot. Use tip 352 and royal icing to pipe a leaf directly on top of wire. Again, push into styrofoam to dry. Remove waxed paper square.

Using a Flower Nail

The flower nail is used as a revolving platform on which you build roses and other flowers. It allows you to work close up, to turn for easy piping and to remove your completed flowers with no damage, ready to dry.

The key to making the flower on the nail is to coordinate the turning of the nail with the formation of a petal.

Attach a square of waxed paper on the flat surface of the flower nail using a dot of icing. Pipe your flower directly on the waxed paper. Hold the flower nail between the thumb and forefinger of your left (right) hand (use other fingers to support nail) and roll it slowly counterclockwise as you press out icing with the decorating bag held in the right (left) hand. Your right (left) hand moves in and out, or up and down, as it holds the decorating bag and tip at just the right angle (in most cases 45°) and keeps the icing flowing at an even speed. After piping, slide the waxed paper with flower off the nail to dry.

Wilton Rose

Practice with Tips: #104, 12

Icing Consistency: Royal or Buttercream—Stiff

Bag Position: Base, 90° Straight Up; Petals, 45° at 4:30 (7:30)

Hold Tip: For Base, Slightly Above Nail; For Petals, Wide End Touching Base

Flower Nail: #7 (Larger Roses) or #9 (Smaller Roses)

The most popular icing flower of all. Pipe two-tone roses for added excitement—pipe the base, center bud and top row petals in one color, then add remaining petals in a contrasting shade.

Note: If you are going to be using your roses immediately on your cake, waxed paper squares are not needed. To remove finished roses, lift off from nail with small scissors, slightly opened. Slide flower from scissors onto cake, using a spatula.

1. Make the rose base, using tip 12 and flower nail No. 7. Hold the bag straight up, the end of tip 12 slightly above the center of your waxed paper-covered flower nail, which is held in your other hand. Using heavy pressure, build up a base, remembering to keep your tip buried as you squeeze.

2. Start to lift the tip higher, gradually raise the tip, and decrease the pressure. Stop pressure, pull up and lift away. The rose base should be $1^1/_2$ times as high as the rose tip opening.
3. Make the center bud, using tip 104. Hold nail containing base in your left (right) hand and bag with rose tip 104 in

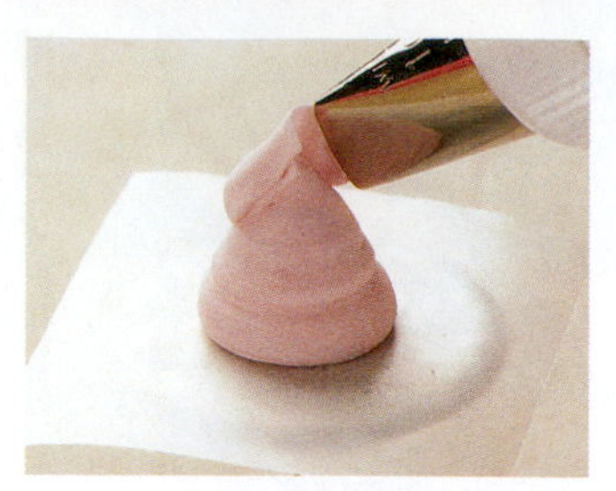

right (left) hand. Bag should be at a 45° angle to the flat surface of the nail and in the 4:30 (7:30) position. The wide end of the tip should touch the cone of the icing base at or slightly below the midpoint, and the narrow end of the tip should point up and angled in over top of base.

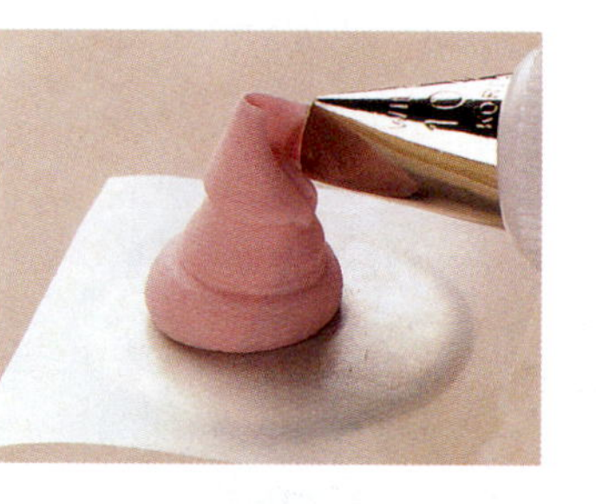

4. Now you must do three things at the same time: squeeze the bag, move the tip and rotate the nail. As you squeeze the bag, move the tip up from the base, forming a ribbon of icing.

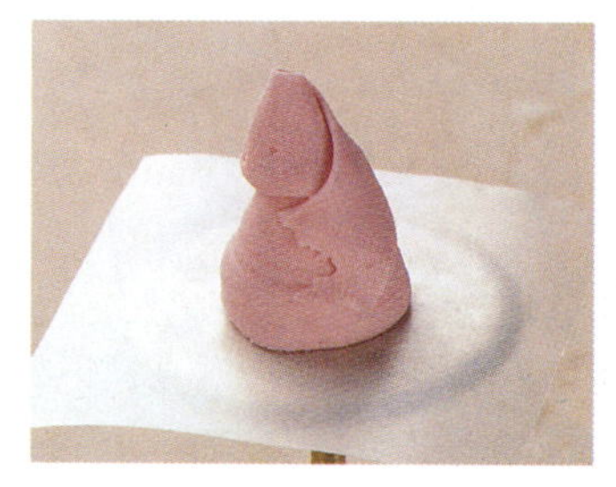

Slowly turn the nail counterclockwise (clockwise for lefties) to bring the ribbon of icing around to overlap at the top of the mound, then back down to starting point. Move your tip straight up and down only; do not loop it around the base.

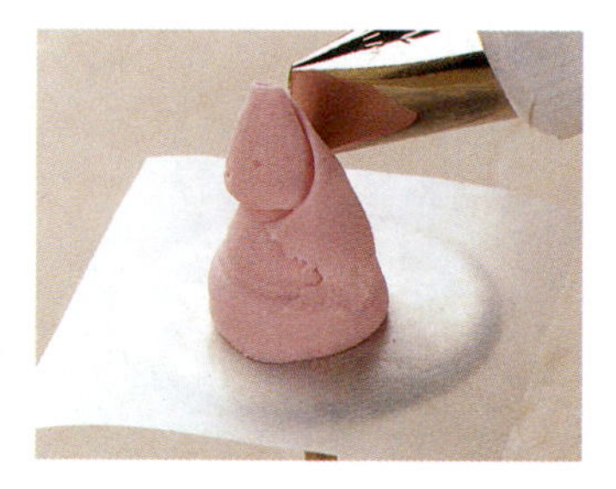

5. Now you have a finished center bud.
6. Make the top row of three petals. Touch the wide end of tip to the midpoint of bud base, narrow end straight up.

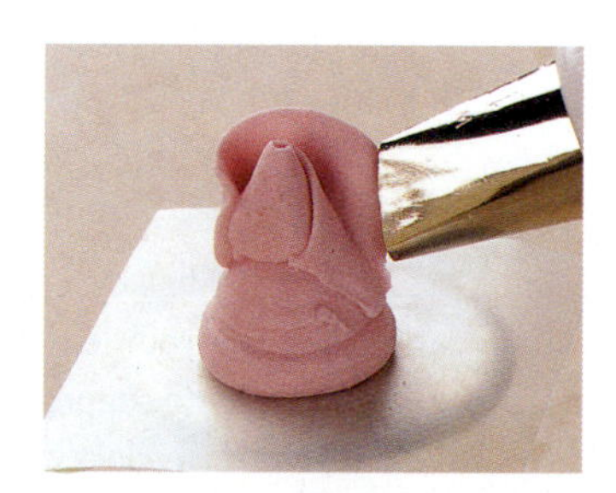

7. Turn nail, keeping wide end of tip on base so that petal will attach. Move tip up and back down to the midpoint of mound, forming the first petal.
8. Start again, slightly behind end of first petal, and squeeze out 2nd petal. Repeat for the third

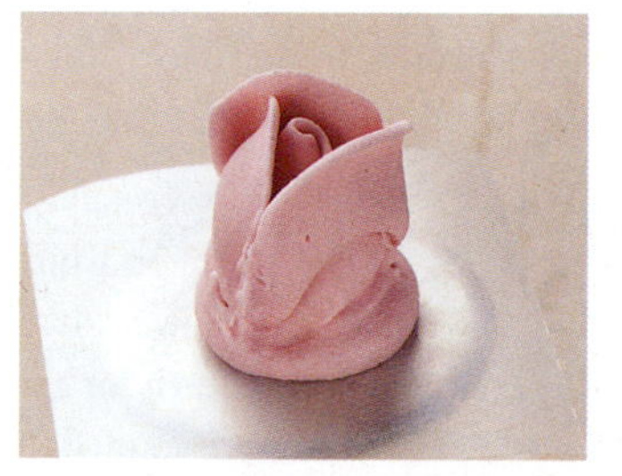

petal, ending by overlapping the starting point of the first petal. Rotate the nail $^1/_3$ turn for each petal.

9. Make the middle row of 5 petals. Touch the wide end of tip slightly below center of a

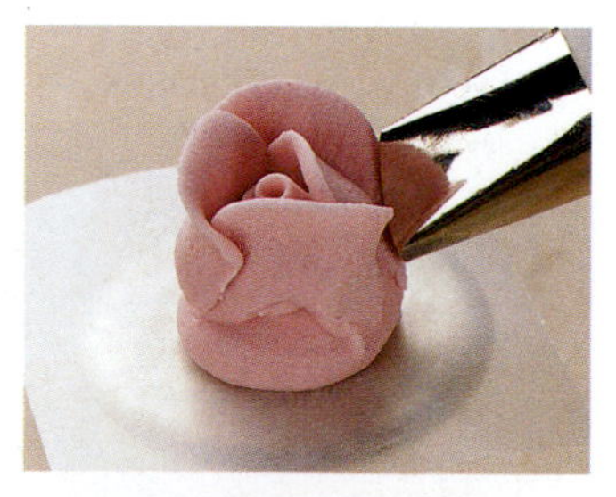

petal in the top row. Angle the narrow end of tip out slightly more than you did for the top row of petals. Squeeze bag and turn nail, moving tip up, then down to form first petal.

10. Repeat for a total of 5 petals, rotating the nail 1/5 turn for each petal.

11. The last petal end should overlap the first's starting point.

12. Make the bottom row of 7 petals. Touch the wide end of tip below the center of middle row petal, again angling the narrow end of tip out a little more. Squeeze

bag and turn nail to end of fingers, moving tip up, then down to form first petal.

13. Repeat for a total of 7 petals, rotating the nail 1/7 turn for each petal.

14. The 7th petal end should overlap the first's starting point. Slip waxed paper and completed rose from nail; attach another square of waxed paper and start again.

15. This is the completed Wilton rose.

BRIMMING WITH ROSES

The world's favorite flower is celebrated in all its glory, underscored with graceful dotted scrolls. Instructions on page 96.

Wild Rose

Practice with Tips: #103, 1

Icing Consistency: Medium Royal Icing

Bag Position: For Petals, 45° at 3:00 (9:00); For Center, 90°

Hold Tip: For Petals, Wide End Lightly Touching Center Of Nail, Narrow End Pointing Out And Raised 1/8 Inch Above Nail Surface; For Centers, Slightly Above Flower

Flower Nail: #7

1. Use tip 103 at a 45° angle. Touch nail with wide end of tip, keeping narrow end just slightly above nail surface. Begin at center of flower nail and squeeze out first petal, turning nail 1/5 turn as you move tip out toward edge of nail. Relax pressure as you return to center of nail, curving tip slightly upward to create a cupped shape. Stop squeezing as wide end touches center of nail and lift up.
2. Repeat step four more times.
3. Pull out tiny stamens with tip 1.

A pretty year-round flower piped about the size of your nail head (number 7). If you prefer a more cupped shape, increase the angle you hold the tip—be sure to dry in flower formers to keep the curved shape.

Apple Blossom

Practice with Tips: #101, 1

Icing Consistency: Medium Royal Icing

Bag Position: For Petals, 45° at 3:00 (9:00); For Center, 90°

Hold Tip: For Petals, Wide End Lightly Touching Center Of Nail, Narrow End Pointing Out And Raised 1/8 Inch Above Nail Surface; For Centers, Slightly Above Flower

Flower Nail: #9

1. Squeeze bag and turn nail as you move tip 1/8 inch out from nail center and back, relaxing pressure as you return to starting point.
2. Repeat to make four more petals.
3. Add five tip 1 dots for center.

This springtime flower is virtually the same as the wild rose, but uses a smaller tip. Pipe apple blossoms about the size of a penny and dry them on flower formers.

Forget-Me-Not

Practice with Tips: #101s, 1

Icing Consistency: Medium Royal Icing

Bag Position: For Petals, 45° at 3:00 (9:00); For Center, 90°

Hold Tip: For Petals, Wide End Of Tip Touching Center Of Nail, Narrow End Pointing Out and Raised 1/8 Inch Above Nail Surface; For Center, Slightly Above Flower

Flower Nail: #9

1. Squeeze bag with light pressure and move tip out 1/16 inch to form first petal. Turn nail, letting spin of nail form petal. Relax pressure as you move tip back to starting point. Stop, lift tip away.
2. Repeat to make four more petals.
3. Add tip 1 dot center.

These tiny spring blossoms can be made in pink, white or blue. They are about half the size of a dime. As with all royal icing flowers, be sure to make more than you need—you don't want to be caught short if flowers break when you are assembling the cake!

SOFT BOUQUET

Wild roses in cool pastels seem to float above this pretty shell border cake. Flowers are actually attached to florist wire, then placed in flower spikes. Instructions on page 100.

SWEET VIOLETS

Richly colored violets are gathered at top and bottom of this round cake. Make royal icing flowers in advance to create a pretty brunch cake fast. Instructions on page 100.

Primrose

Practice with Tips: #103, 14, 1

Icing Consistency: Medium Royal Icing

Bag Position: For Petals, 45° at 3:00 (9:00); For Center, 90°

Hold Tip: For Petals, Wide End Of Tip Lightly Touching Center Of Nail, Narrow End Pointing Out and Raised ¼ Inch Above Nail Surface; For Center, Slightly Above Flower

Flower Nail: #7

1. Squeeze bag and move tip out 1/4 inch using a "curve, dip, curve" motion to form first heart-shaped petal while turning nail in opposite direction. (Move tip out 1/4 inch, then in 1/8 inch and back out.) Relax pressure as you return to starting point.
2. Repeat procedure for remaining four petals.
3. Pipe tip 14 center star with tip 1 dot. Let dry.

The key to forming its heart-shaped petals is perfecting a "curve-dip-curve" motion as you spin the flower nail.

Violet

Practice with Tips: #59s/59° or 101s, 1

Icing Consistency: Medium Royal Icing

Bag Position: For Petals, 45° at 3:00 (9:00); For Center, 90°

Hold Tip: For Petals, Wide End Of Tip Touching Nail Center, Narrow End Pointed 1/8 Inch Away From Nail Surface; For Center, Slightly Above Flower

Flower Nail: #9

1. Make a 3/4 inch long petal: Squeeze bag and turn nail 1/5 of circle as you move tip 1/8 inch in from nail center and back, relaxing pressure as you return to starting point. Repeat to make two more petals.
2. Add two 1/4 inch base petals.
3. Add two tip 1 center dots

The violet is an ideal "filler" flower. Use it to give an abundant look to all kinds of floral cakes. It looks beautiful in white and yellow as well as violet.

Pansy

Practice with Tips: #104, 1

Icing Consistency: Medium Royal Icing

Bag Position: For Petals, 45° at 3:00 (9:00); For Center, 90°

Hold Tip: For Petals, Wide End Of Tip Lightly Touching Nail Center, Narrow End Pointing Out And Raised 1/4 Inch Above Nail Surface; For Center, Hold Slightly Above Flower.

Flower Nail: #7 or #9

1. Pipe two back petals, squeezing and moving tip out to edge of nail. Turn nail slowly while squeezing, relax pressure as you return to nail center. Repeat to form second back petal. Use the same sequence to add two shorter petals atop the first two.
2. Squeeze out a base petal that equals the width of the back petals, using a back and forth hand motion for a ruffled effect.
3. Use a fine artist's brush to paint thinned icing color veins, edging and highlights to flower after it has dried. Add tip 1 string loop centers.

Color options abound for this robust flower. Petals can be dark blue, orange, red or white, highlighted with a complementary color. Add multi-tones by using a striped bag or by painting in colors at the flower's center or edge with a fine artist's brush dipped in a small amount of clear vanilla which has been tinted with icing color.

Bachelor Button

Practice with Tips: #1, 5, 16

Icing Consistency: Medium Royal Icing

Bag Position: For Mound And Center Stamens, 90°; For Star Petals, 45° at 3:00 (9:00)

Hold Tip: For Mound, Slightly Above Center Of Nail; For Center Stamens, Lightly Touching Center Of Mound; For Star Petals, Tip Touching Edge Of Mound

Flower Nail: #7

1. Hold bag at 90° angle to flower nail, lightly touching surface. Pipe tip 5 dot base.
2. Pipe a cluster of short pull-out dots in the center using tip 1.
3. Using tip 16, cover the remainder of mound with stars. Start at base, then work toward center.

This handsome flower is an excellent choice on men's cakes and in summer floral arrangements. Bachelor buttons look terrific in blue, white, pink or lavender.

Chrysanthemum

Practice with Tips: #5, 81

Icing Consistency: Stiff Royal Icing

Bag Position: For Mound, 90°; For Petals, 45° at 3:00 (9:00)

Hold Tip: For Mound, 1/4 Inch Above Center; For Petals, Curved Side Up

1. Hold bag at 90° angle to flower nail. Pipe a tip 5 mound of icing on nail center.
2. Use tip 81 and hold bag at a 45° angle to outer base edge of mound, with half moon opening of tip pointing up. Squeeze row of 1/2 inch long cupped base petals, pull up slightly as you release pressure to form petals.
3. Add second row of shorter petals atop and in between those in first row. Repeat procedure between those in second row. Repeat procedure, making each additional row of petals shorter than the previous row.

A fall tradition, with a sunburst of sharply-defined petals. You'll see them in rich, warm autumn colors like rust, golden yellow and terra cotta as well as pink and white.

Carnation

Practice with Tips: #12, 150 (104 Is Optional)

Icing Consistency: Stiff Royal Icing

Bag Position: For Mound, 90°; For Petals, 45° at 4:30 (7:30)

Hold Tip: For Mound, Slightly Above Surface; For Petals, One End Of Tip Touching Mound, The Other End Straight Up

Flower Nail: #7

1. Hold bag at 90° angle to flower nail. Use stiff royal icing. Pipe tip 12 ball on flower nail.
2. Using tip 150 (104 optional), pipe several upstanding petals in center of ball with a jiggling up and down motion, then circle them with ruffled petals.
3. As you continue piping rows of petals to cover ball, turn narrow end of tip farther out. Pipe last row of petals at base of flower with tip straight out.

Think of a carnation as row upon row of ruffles piped over a center mound. It's a welcome flower in any season—try it with a striped bag (stripe on narrow tip side) for lovely color variation.

Daisy

Practice with Tips: #104, 5

Icing Consistency: Medium Royal Icing

Bag Position: For Petals, 45° at 3:00 (9:00); For Center, 90°

Hold Tip: For Petals, Wide End Lightly Touching 1/4 Inch Away From Center Of Nail, Narrow End Pointing Out To Outer Edge; For Center, Hold Slightly Above Flower

Flower Nail: #7

1. Dot center of flower nail with icing as guide for flower center. Starting at any point near outer edge of nail, squeeze and move tip towards center icing dot. Stop pressure, pull tip away.
2. Repeat for a total of 12 or more petals.
3. Add tip 5 flower center and press to flatten. For pollen effect, dampen your finger, dip in crushed Cake Sparkles, then press on center.

Try these color combinations on your daisies—yellow petals with yellow or blue centers, violet or blue petals with yellow centers, peach petals with orange centers. Highlight the centers with Wilton Cake Sparkles or colored sugars which are extra fine texture.

Daffodil

Practice with Tips: #104, 3, 1

Icing Consistency: Medium Royal Icing

Bag Position: For Petals, 45° at 3:00 (9:00); For Center, 90°

Hold Bag: For Petals, Wide End Of Tip Lightly Touching Center Of Nail, Narrow End Pointing Out And Raised 1/4 Inch Above Nail Surface; For Center, Slightly Above Flower

Flower Nail: #7

1. Squeeze and as you turn nail, move tip out about 1/2 inch and back to center of nail to form petal.
2. Repeat for 5 more petals.
3. Dip fingers in cornstarch and pinch ends of petals to form points.
4. For center throat, pipe a spiral of tip 3 string circles and top with tip 1 zigzag.

The sequence of piping the daffodil is the same for both the narcissus and the jonquil. The narcissus is a smaller flower with white tip 103 petals, a yellow throat and a red trim atop the throat. The jonquil is also smaller than the daffodil, with white tip 103 petals and a yellow center. Dry all of these flowers on medium flower formers.

SUNSHINE FLOURISHES

A generous ruffle holds gorgeous puffed carnations on a cake that will brighten everyone's day. Instructions on page 99.

Using a Lily Nail

The lily nail helps you achieve deeply cupped flowers. You use different size nails for small and large flowers—nails range from $\frac{1}{2}$ to $2\frac{1}{2}$ inches in diameter and are available in one-piece and two-piece styles.

To produce flowers in your lily nail, it must first be lined with aluminum foil. This makes removal of the flower from the nail possible! To prevent the foil in your lily nail from moving when piping flowers, squeeze a dab of icing in the nail before adding the foil.

For one-piece nails: Line with a 2-inch square of aluminum foil, pressing foil down smoothly. For two-piece nails: Place a 2 inch square of aluminum foil in the bottom half of the lily nail. Gently press the top half down into the foil, lift off. Some flowers require a shallower foil cup. For those flowers, push foil halfway into the nail.

Hold the lily nail between the thumb and forefinger on your left (right) hand and roll it slowly counterclockwise (clockwise) as you press out icing with the decorating bag held in the right (left) hand. Remove the foil cup with flower and set aside to dry.

Lily

Practice with Tips: #68, 14
Icing Consistency: Stiff Royal Icing
Bag Position: For Petals, 45° at 3:00 (9:00); For Center, 90°
Hold Tip: For Petals, Lightly Touching Surface of Nail, Wide Opening Parallel To Surface; For Center, Slightly Above Flower

This glorious springtime flower looks its best when petals are more pointed. If your petals split as you're piping, widen the tip slightly by inserting a thin spatula into the opening. Or, add a teaspoon of piping gel to one cup of stiff royal icing.

1. Line $1\frac{5}{8}$ inch lily nail with foil. Use tip 68. Touch center well of nail with tip and squeeze, pulling petal up and over edge of foil cup. Decrease pressure as you reach end of petal and hesitate before you stop pressure and pull tip away, drawing petal to a point.
2. Pipe two more petals.
3. Pipe three more petals in between open spaces.
4. Add tip 14 star center and push in stamens.

Petunia

Practice with Tips: #103, 16
Icing Consistency: Stiff Royal Icing
Bag Position: For Petals, 45° at 3:00 (9:00); For Center, 90°
Hold Tip: For Petals, Wide End Touching Surface With Narrow End Slightly Lifted; For Center Star, Slightly Above Flower

To ensure the proper spacing of petals, try this trick: Pipe dots of icing with tip 103 on top of the lily nail, dividing it in fifths—visualize the points of a star. Pipe each petal centered over its dot.

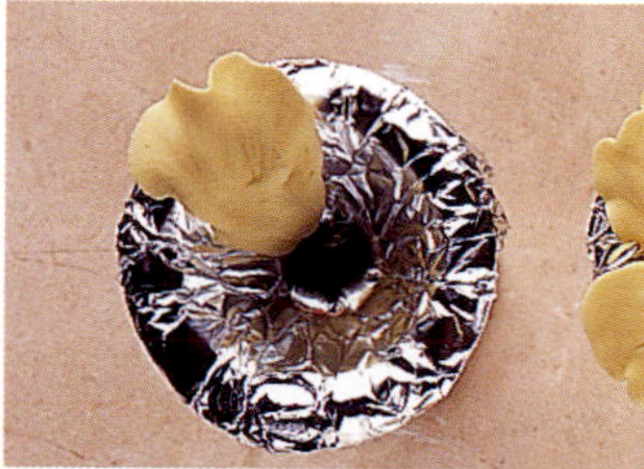

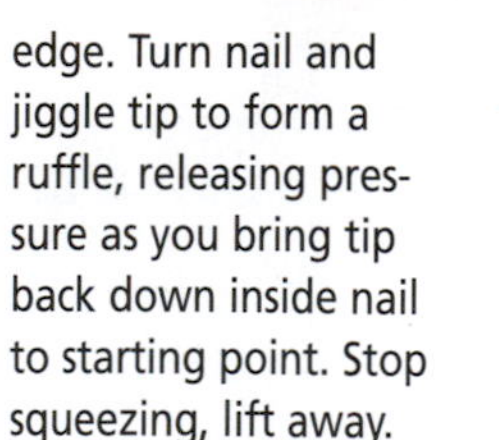

1. Line $1\frac{5}{8}$ inch lily nail with foil. Use tip 103. Insert tip into the cup of the nail, position wide end of tip down. Squeeze inside the nail and move up to outer edge. Turn nail and jiggle tip to form a ruffle, releasing pressure as you bring tip back down inside nail to starting point. Stop squeezing, lift away.
2. Repeat to make four more petals.
3. Smooth bases of petals together at center of flower with a dampened decorator brush. Using light pressure, pipe tip 16 star in center.
4. Insert five stamens in center, sprinkle with Cake Sparkles.

Morning Glory

Practice with Tips: #104,103,2,1
Icing Consistency: Stiff Royal Icing
Bag Position: For Ruffled Cup, 45° at 3:00 (9:00); For Stamen, 90°
Hold Tip: For Inner Flower Cup, Wide And Narrow Ends Touching Surface; For Petals, Wide End Touching Top Of Nail

When you are smoothing together the edges of your inner cup and ruffled cup, don't use too much water. Touch the brush to your hand before applying to remove excess water.

1. Line $1\frac{5}{8}$ inch lily nail with foil. Position wide end of tip down in nail. Using tip 104 and white icing, pipe a shallow cup within the nail. Pipe a second cup slightly above the first. Smooth with a damp brush.
2. Using tinted icing and tip 103, pipe a ruffled cup slightly above the white inner cup, increasing pressure in five places to form points.
3. With dampened decorator brush, blend tinted icing into white center. Next, brush white icing up to form a star shape.
4. Using tip 1 and thinned white icing, pipe five lines from base of flower to edge. Pipe tip 2 center stamen using yellow icing.

Poinsettia

Practice with Tips: #352, 2
Icing Consistency: Stiff Royal Icing
Bag Position: For Petals, 45° at 3:00 (9:00); 90° For Center
Hold Tip: For Petals, Pointed End Touching Nail; For Center, Hold Slightly Above Surface

The classic Christmas flower may be piped in white, pink or red. It's one of the more shallow flowers you will pipe in the lily nail; don't push your foil more than halfway into the cup.

1. Position foil halfway in $1\frac{5}{8}$ inch lily nail. Insert tip 352 into lily nail. Squeeze hard and pipe leaf-shaped petal just over edge of foil cup; relax pressure, stop and pull away. Pipe two more petals, dividing the nail into thirds.
2. Add three more petals in the open spaces.
3. Add six smaller leaf-shaped petals on top and between the larger ones.
4. Add seven tip 2 dots in a circle for center.

Bluebell

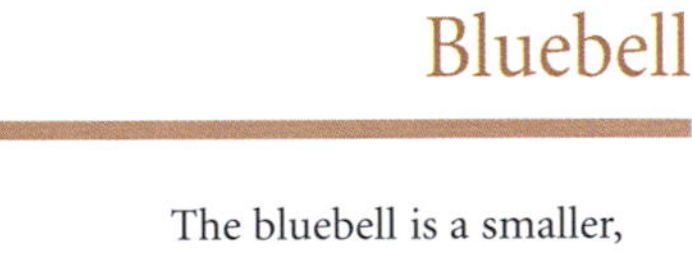

Practice with Tips: #66, 2
Icing Consistency: Stiff Royal Icing
Bag Position: 45° at 3:00 (9:00)
Hold Tip: Lightly Touching Surface Of Nail, Wide Opening Parallel To Surface

The bluebell is a smaller, slightly shallower version of the lily, done in the smaller $1\frac{1}{4}$ inch nail. Bluebells may be piped in white, pink and yellow or traditional blue.

Note: Stamens are not to be eaten.

1. Line $1\frac{1}{4}$ inch nail with foil. Using tip 66, pipe three $\frac{3}{4}$ inch long petals, pulling only to top of nail.
2. Add three more petals in the open spaces.
3. Add tip 2 dot for center and insert three short stamens.

Leaves

Practice with Tips: #352, 67, 366

Icing Consistency: Buttercream—Thinned with Corn Syrup

Bag Position: 45° at 6:00

Hold Tip: Lightly Touching Surface; Wide Opening Parallel to Surface

Basic Leaf— Tip #352

Veined Leaf— Tip #67

Large Leaf— Tip #366
Use large coupler

These three leaves are all made following the same sequence.

Squeeze hard to build up the base, and at the same time, lift the tip slightly.

Relax pressure as you pull the tip toward you, drawing the leaf to a point.

Stop squeezing and lift away.

Practice with Tip: #67

Icing Consistency: Buttercream—Thinned with Corn Syrup

Bag Position: 45° at 6:00

Hold Tip: Lightly Touching Surface; Wide Opening Parallel to Surface

Ruffled Leaf

Hold bag at 45° angle to surface. Squeeze, hold tip in place to let icing fan out into base, then move tip up and down to create ruffles. Relax, stop pressure and pull tip away.

Extended Leaf

Hold bag at 45° to surface. Squeeze, move tip along to desired length. Relax, stop pressure and pull tip away.

Stand-up Leaf

Hold bag at a 45° angle to surface. Touch tip lightly to surface and squeeze, holding tip in place as icing fans out to form base. Relax and stop pressure as you pull tip up and away.

Vines

Practice with Tip: #3

Icing Consistency: Thin

Bag Position: 45° at 3:00 (9:00)

Hold Tip: Lightly Touching Surface

1. Touch your tip lightly to the surface as you start to squeeze, then lift slightly above the surface as you draw out the stem.
2. Move tip gently up and down to form "hills and valleys." To end the line, stop squeezing, and pull the tip along the surface.
3. Add secondary curved stems, starting at main stem, stopping pressure as you pull to a point.

BERRY BONANZA

Berries never looked fresher. Raspberries are coated with finely crushed Cake Sparkles, then added to the vine and leaf decorated cake. Instructions on page 100.

Holly Leaf

Practice with Tip: #70

Icing Consistency: Thin Royal

Bag Position: 45° at 6:00

Hold Tip: Lightly Touching Surface; Wide Opening Parallel to Surface

Flower Nail: No. 7

1. Using tip 70 and holding bag at a 45° angle to surface at 6:00, pipe a basic leaf.

2. While icing is wet, pull out tiny points around edge with a toothpick.

3. Let dry on flower formers for a curved look. Do not make directly on cake.

Violet Leaf

Practice with Tip: #104

Icing Consistency: Medium Royal

Bag Position: 45° at 6:00

Hold Tip: Wide End of Tip Lightly Touching Surface of Nail

Flower Nail: No. 7

1. Squeeze with medium pressure, using a jiggling motion. Slide tip out about 1/4 inch as you turn the nail.

2. Relax pressure, move back to starting point.

3. Stop pressure, pull away.

Fern

Practice with Tips: #67, 1

Icing Consistency: Thin Buttercream

Bag Position: Slightly Less Than 90° at 6:00

Hold Tip: Lightly Touching Surface; Wide Opening Parallel To Surface

1. Starting at the bottom, using heavy pressure, hold bag stationary and pipe a tip 67 fern leaf. Working towards top, continue to pipe tip 67 leaves.

2. As you approach top, gradually decrease pressure with each fern leaf.

3. Add tip 1 dots and curled frond to complete.

A JOY TO BEHOLD

A festive holly and poinsettia wreath heralds the holiday season. The perfect centerpiece for your Christmas buffet. Instructions on page 101.

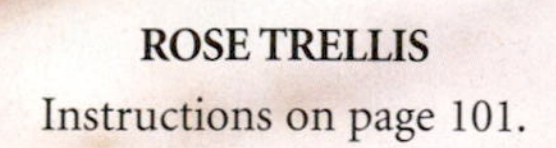

ROSE TRELLIS

Instructions on page 101.

Fondant

Discover versatile fondant icing—it's more than just a perfectly smooth cake covering. The dough-like consistency of fondant makes it the perfect medium for creating ruffles and braids, stately molded accents, distinctive borders, fun trims and beautiful flowers. Decorators agree that fondant is an icing that is truly easy to work with. Once you try fondant, it will soon become one of your favorite ways to decorate!

Covering the Cake with Rolled Fondant

1. Prepare cake by covering with buttercream icing.

2. Before rolling out fondant, knead until it is a workable consistency. If fondant is sticky, knead in a little confectioners' sugar. Lightly dust smooth work surface and rolling pin with confectioners' sugar to prevent sticking.

3. Roll out fondant sized to your cake (see sidebar). Roll fondant with rolling pin, lifting and moving as you roll. Add more confectioners' sugar if necessary.

4. Gently lift fondant over rolling pin, or lift with the support of both hands, taking care not to tear it with your fingernails. Position on cake.

5. Shape fondant to sides of cake with Easy-Glide Smoother. We recommend using the Smoother because the warmth of your hands can affect fondant. Use the straight edge of Smoother to mark fondant at base of cake; trim off using a sharp knife or pizza cutter.

6. Smooth and shape fondant on cake using palm of hand or Easy-Glide Smoother. Beginning in the middle of the cake top, move the Easy-Glide Smoother outward and down the sides to smooth and shape fondant to cake and remove air bubbles. If an air bubble appears, pop it with a pin and smooth area again.

To determine the diameter you need to roll fondant for covering your cake: measure opposite sides and top of cake across center; roll out fondant to that size, 1/4 inch thick. For example, an 8 inch, two-layer cake, with two sides each 4 inches, equals 16 inches diameter. For simple, accurate measuring, roll out the fondant on top of the Cake Dividing Wheel included in the Wilton Cake Dividing Set.

More Helpful Hints for Fondant:

In general, the less height on your cake, the easier it will be to cover with rolled fondant. Individual sized desserts, such as petits fours are the easiest of all to cover.

When rolling fondant, it is extremely important to remember to lift and move it several times. You must keep fondant from sticking to your rolling surface, or it will tear when you try to lift it up.

Covering Large Rounds

1. Cover cake with buttercream icing. Roll out fondant sized to your cake.

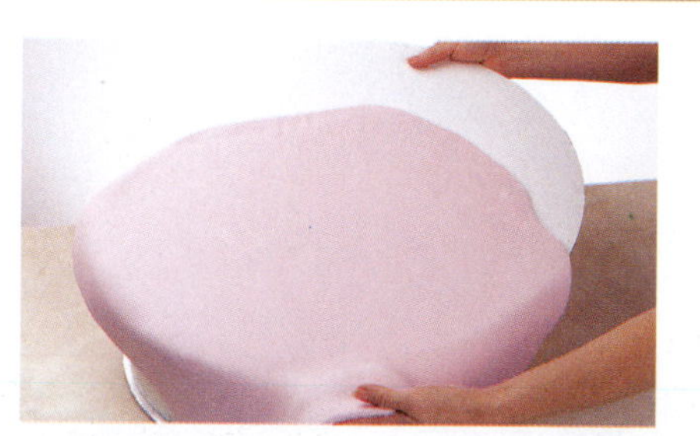

2. Slide a large cake circle that has been dusted with confectioners' sugar under the rolled fondant. Lift the circle and the fondant and position over cake. Gently shake the circle to slide the fondant off the board and into position on the cake. Smooth and trim as described above.

Rounds are easy to cover with fondant. But what about other geometric shaped cakes? On squares or hearts, pull the corner flaps gently out and downward, then smooth to avoid creases. On petals, smooth fondant downward in petal divisions for complete coverage.

LOVE INTERTWINING

The pretty fondant rope frames a spray of delicate blossoms on a cake ideal for Valentine's Day or any romantic occasion. Instructions on page 101.

Covering Shaped Cakes

1. Prepare cake by covering with a thin layer of buttercream icing. Roll out fondant and cover cake. Smooth fondant over details on cake and trim at bottom border.

2. Now you will add details (facial features and paws): Dust inside of pan with confectioners' sugar to prevent sticking. Mold fondant into detailed areas of pan, press to smooth and carefully remove from pan.

3. Position molded fondant pieces on cake. To attach to fondant cake, brush back with water. Fondant trims can be placed directly on buttercream cakes. Finish decorating using buttercream icing.

Use the cake pan as a pattern when rolling out fondant to cover unusually-shaped cakes. Measure pan at widest and longest areas, add 2 or 3 inches along sides for adequate coverage.

Fondant Tools

Working with fondant icing has never been easier. Whether you're covering a cake or shaping fondant decorations, there's a tool that will help.

Create realistic floral bouquets, accents and blossoms using specially-designed fondant **Cutter Sets**. An **Ejector Tool** allows you the ease of one-hand operation when cutting and attaching flowers to cakes. Look for distinctive cutters to highlight bridal and anniversary cakes, including orchids, stephanotis, forget-me-nots and roses.

Embossers imprint elegant designs on fondant quickly and easily. Imprinted designs can also be painted with clear vanilla tinted with icing colors for an exciting effect.

Confectionery Tools help you shape, imprint and stencil fondant to create lifelike confectionery flowers. A good set might include Dogbone, Umbrella, Shell, Ball and Veining tools.

A **Roller** that fits comfortably in the palm of your hand is a great asset when rolling small pieces of fondant to a smooth, even thickness, essential for cutting flower petals, leaves, accents and designs.

Mold stunning fondant plaques, medallions, accents and border treatments using **Fondant Molds**. Simply press fondant into molds and release, then attach fondant to cake. Great for candy and butter molding too.

Marbleizing

1. Knead fondant until soft and pliable. Using a toothpick, add dots of color randomly to fondant.

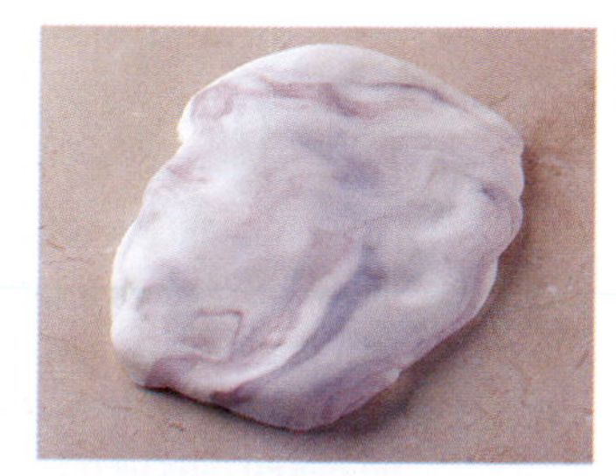

2. Knead fondant slightly until color begins to blend in, creating marbleized streaks.

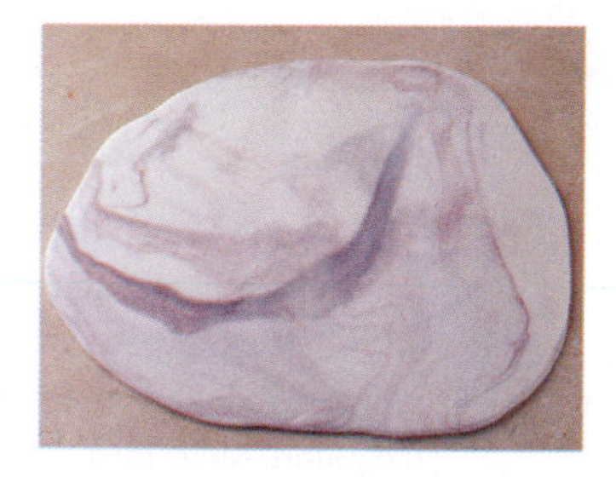

3. Roll out to desired shape.

The simple beauty of covering a cake with marbleized fondant is that all you need to do is add a border and simple decorations, such as flowers, and your decorating is complete. Don't knead the color into the fondant too much; distinctive streaks of color should be seen.

Fondant Molding

You can create pretty shapes with fondant using just about any type of mold. Fondant or candy molds work well as do shaped cake pans. To remove molded shapes, use a craft knife or a veining tool.

1. Lightly dust mold with cornstarch or confectioners' sugar. Shake out excess. Knead fondant until soft. Break off a small piece to fit mold.

2. Press gently into mold to flatten. Push fondant to edges of mold with flat edge of spatula.

3. Turn mold over to release or use spatula edge to gently lift fondant out of mold.

Fondant Ruffles

Excellent for baby accents—from bassinets to bibs. Ruffles are also a nice way to finish the sleeves and neckline of doll dresses.

1. Roll out fondant and cut into sections 3/4 inch wide.

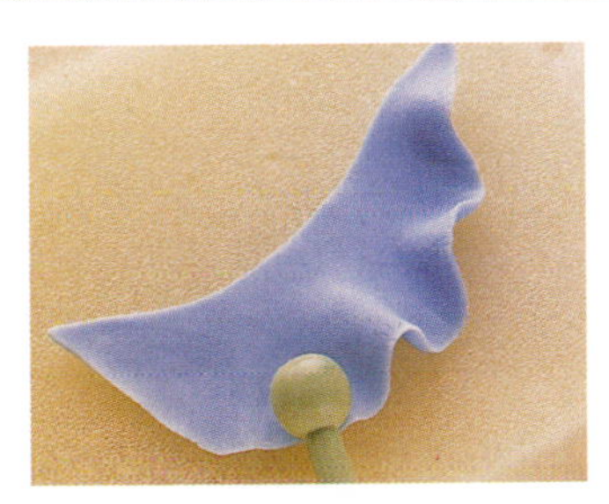

2. Form ruffles with ball tool from Confectionery Tool Set dipped in cornstarch; gently roll end of tool along one long flat edge of fondant.

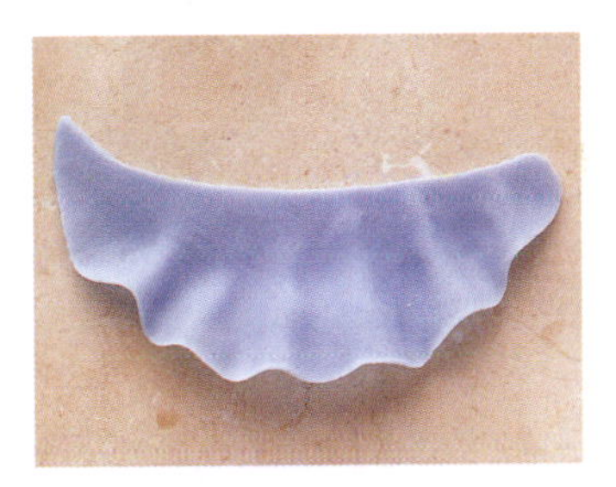

3. Use decorator brush and a small amount of water to attach the plain edge of fondant to cake.

Brush Embroidery

Gentle brushstrokes of icing, piped directly on your cake, set a soft, romantic tone for wedding and anniversary cakes. Be sure to brush the design immediately after piping your outlines—the technique won't work on dry icing.

1. Make a flower pattern using a gum paste flower cutter, then outline one area at a time with thin consistency buttercream icing.

2. Before each outline can dry, immediately brush out lines of icing towards center of pattern area using a dampened decorator brush. Work in short, quick strokes.

3. Clean brush in water after brushing each flower, to create distinct lines of icing.

Fondant Cut-Outs

There's no limit to the shapes you can add to your fondant cake! Use cookie cutters as we have here, or trace a design with a toothpick, then cut with a craft knife.

1. Roll out fondant 1/8 inch thick.

2. Position cutter on fondant and press straight down without twisting.

3. Remove fondant cut-out using the end of a spatula.

Inlays

Blocks of color to brighten any celebration! Be gentle when cutting pieces from the cake—you don't want to break the cake surface.

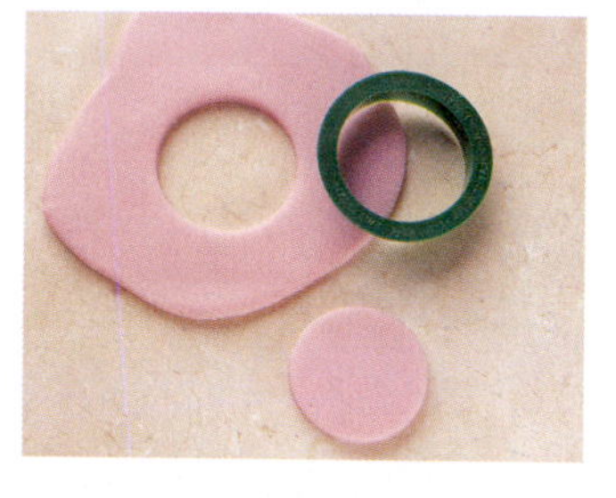

1. Using a cookie or gum paste cutter, or the end of a decorating tip, cut out shapes from a piece of rolled fondant in a different color from your fondant-covered cake.

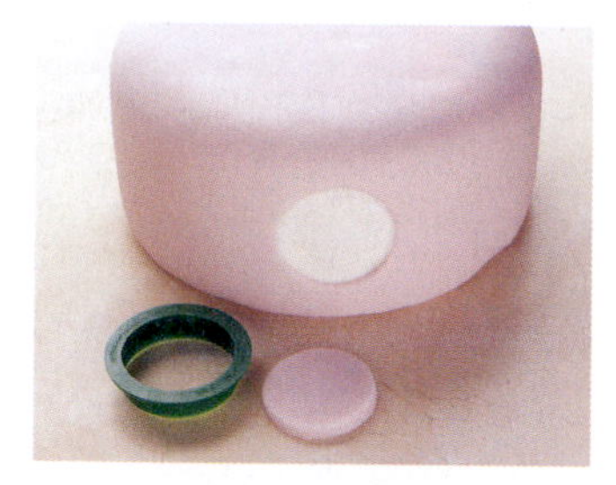

2. Cut the same size shape from your cake. Remove the cut piece from your cake.

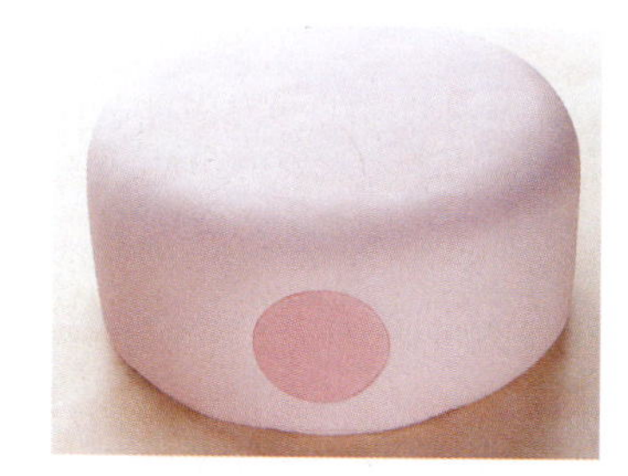

3. Position the different color shape. Smooth with finger dipped in cornstarch or with an Easy-Glide Smoother to blend edges.

Blossoms

These tiny cupped flowers can accent the brush embroidery flowers on page 77—just attach a blossom with buttercream to make a pretty center.

1. Roll out fondant about 1/8 inch thick, on surface dusted with cornstarch. Cut with blossom cutter.

2. Remove excess fondant around blossoms, transfer blossoms one at a time to foam square. Use ball tool from Confectionery Tool Set to make a cupped shape blossom, by depressing tool in center of flower.

3. Pipe a tip 2 dot flower center using thinned royal icing.

POLKA-DOT PARTY!

Bright circles of fondant echo the fun balloons which top this great fondant cake. Use the easy inlay technique. Instructions on page 101.

Cutting Fondant Shapes Using Ejectors

It's easy to cut pretty little blossoms, then eject them right on your cake. Great for petit fours and cupcakes. If you wish, pipe a dot of buttercream or roll a tiny fondant ball for the flower center.

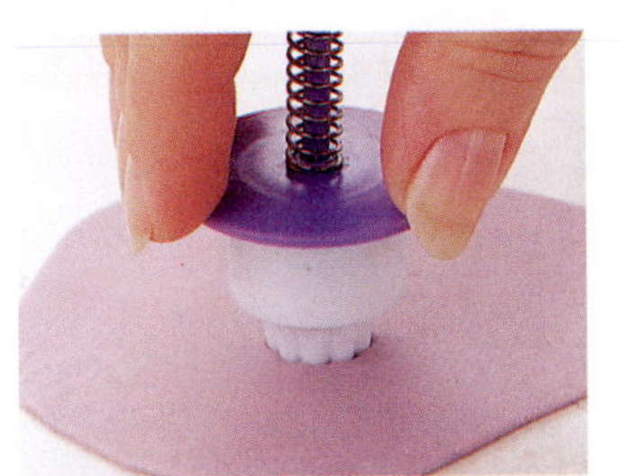

1. Roll fondant to 1/8 inch thick. Position ejector on fondant and press down to cut fondant; twist gently, but do not push plunger. Lift ejector off fondant.

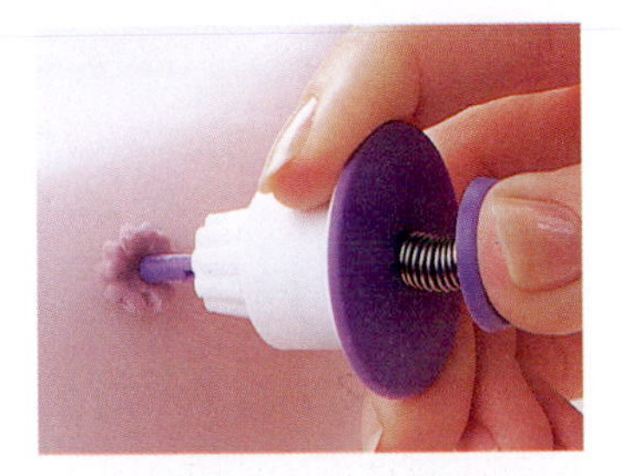

2. Pipe a dot of icing on cake where fondant will be positioned, or brush area lightly with water.

3. Position ejector on cake and lightly push plunger with thumb to attach fondant to cake.

Fondant Rope

Here's why decorators love to work with fondant—a rope is so much easier to shape with your hands in fondant than to pipe in buttercream icing.

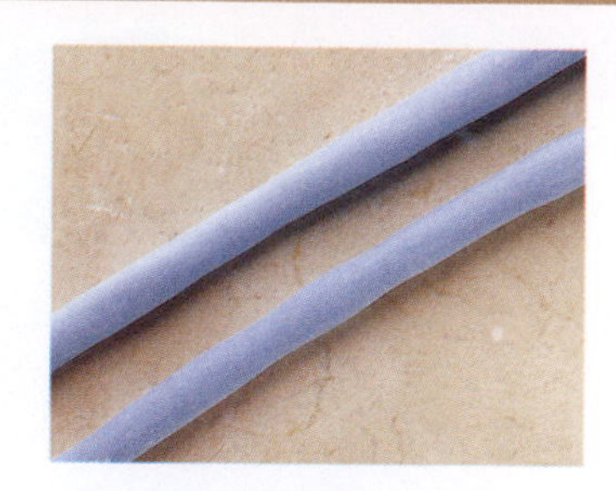

1. Roll fondant into 1/4 inch diameter pieces using palms of hands. You will need two pieces the same length. Lay the pieces side by side, and gently press together at one end to join.

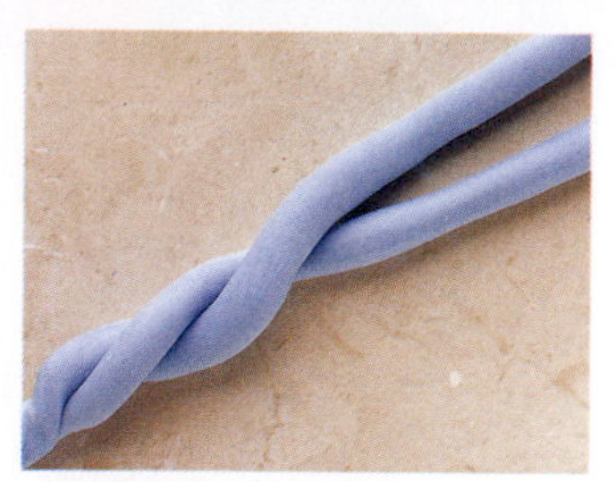

2. Holding the joined end stationary, twist other end 2-3 complete turns.

3. Attach rope to cake using a decorator brush and water. Moisten area slightly and position rope, pressing ends lightly to secure.

Fondant Braid

A great textured look for bottom borders or to highlight western-look rope and floral cakes.

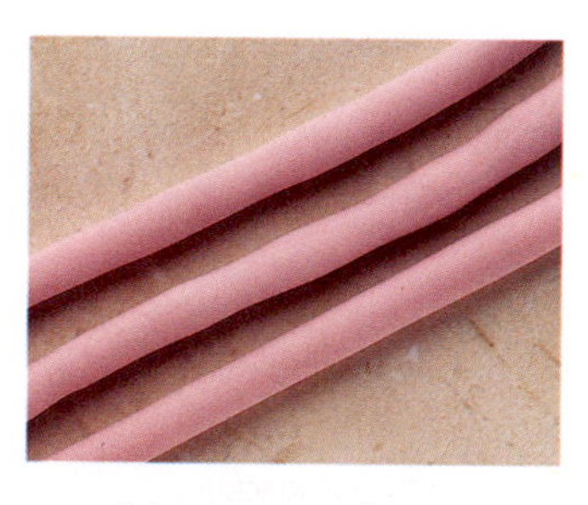

1. Roll fondant into 1/4 inch diameter pieces using palms of hands. You will need three pieces the same length. Lay the pieces side by side, and gently press together at one end to join.

2. Move the fondant length positioned at the right between the left and middle lengths. Now, position the left length between the middle and right. Continue in this manner until the entire length is braided.

3. Gently press the three ends together to secure. Attach the braid to cake using decorator brush and water. Moisten area slightly and position, pressing lightly to secure.

Fondant Streamers

Create your own festive party streamers for a fun New Year's or birthday celebration! It's fun to add streamers on dessert plates or trays for that extra dash of color.

1. Roll out fondant 1/8 inch thick. Cut into thin strips.

2. Wrap strip around a dowel rod. To retain shape, let dry on dowel rod for a few hours.

3. Slide off curl from dowel rod.

Fondant Ribbon Rose

Quicker and easier than piping icing flowers, these fondant roses can be placed directly on your cake after you roll them. Moisten cake area slightly with a damp decorator brush to attach. Fondant leaves or piped icing leaves will highlight these roses.

1. Roll out 1/8 inch thick strip of fondant 2 inches x 5 inches.

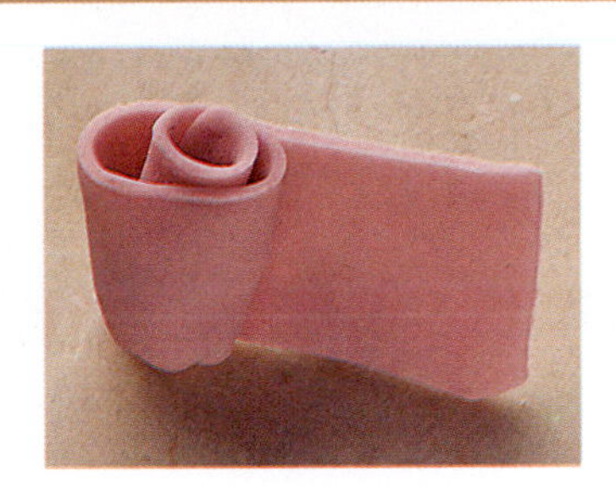

2. Begin rolling lightly from one end, gradually loosening roll as flower gets larger. You will be rolling three complete turns. Cut off end and fold edge under.

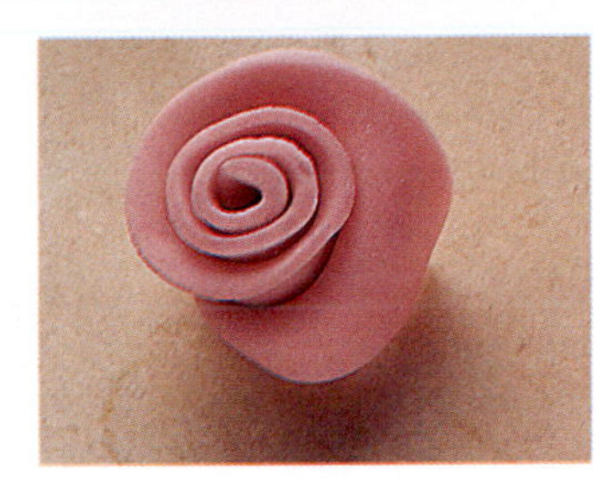

3. Trim flower so it is 3/4 to 1 inch high.

Sponging on Fondant

Textured highlighting makes a great backdrop for flowers, stringwork, ruffles and shells. It's an easy-to-create design that looks impressive on shower, wedding and party cakes.

1. Thin buttercream icing. Dampen a new sponge and lightly dip into icing. Using a quick pulling motion, blot icing on cake surface to produce a spackled effect. Different spackled effects can be achieved using crushed waxed paper or paper towel.

Painting on Fondant

From flowers to family crests, painted designs give your cake personality! The Vanilla Extract added to the icing color helps the color to dry fast.

1. Tint a small amount of clear vanilla extract with icing color. Using a decorator brush, paint stems using a continuous, flowing motion. To prevent the colors from running, do not let brush get too wet.

2. Paint leaves using heavy to light pressure.

3. Complete design and let dry.

Fondant Draping

Inspired by opulent fabric, fondant drapes beautify side borders or skirt accents. Be certain not to roll the fondant too thin, as the weight of the drape may tear the fondant at the ends.

1. Roll out fondant to 1/8 inch thickness. For an 8 inch round cake, cut a 4 x 3 inch rectangle. You will need 8 rectangles; work one at a time so that fondant doesn't dry out.

2. Immediately gather the short ends and pinch together to form drapes.

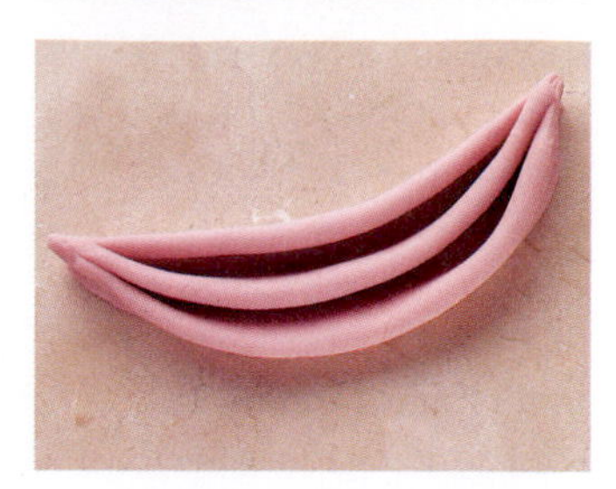

3. Attach drapes to cake by brushing back with water.

Bows/Loops

Every pretty package needs a bow—make it simple or with lots of fancy loops! For an elegant look, edge the fondant strips with a pastry crimper wheel before folding bows.

1. Roll fondant 1/8 inch thick. Make a practice bow using these measurements; once you have mastered these steps, modify the measurements for your own cake design: Cut two strips 1 inch wide x 6 inches long for loops and one length 1 inch wide x 2 inches long for center.

2. Make two loops: Fold strip over to form a loop, aligning ends. Brush ends with a damp brush. Pinch ends slightly to secure. Stand loops upright on side to dry. Make a bow center: Wrap length around your finger to create a loop; brush area to be seamed with a damp brush; overlap the ends slightly and press together to secure. Stand bow center on its side to dry.

3. Insert the ends of two loops into center; secure with dots of icing if necessary and position on cake.

A SWEET PRESENT

Wrap up a great cake with an easy-to-shape fondant bow. Tiny blossoms made with the Ejector complete the look. Instructions on page 101.

Fondant Rose

People marvel at the realism of these roses! They also work well in candy clay or marzipan. To make a stem for a single rose, roll a thin log of green fondant and attach.

1. Using a 3/4 inch diameter ball of fondant, mold a cone base approximately 1 1/2 inch high.

2. Roll a 3/8 inch diameter ball of fondant.

3. Flatten this ball into a circular petal about 1/4 inch thick on bottom and thin on the top. Make about the diameter of a nickel. Make several petals this size.

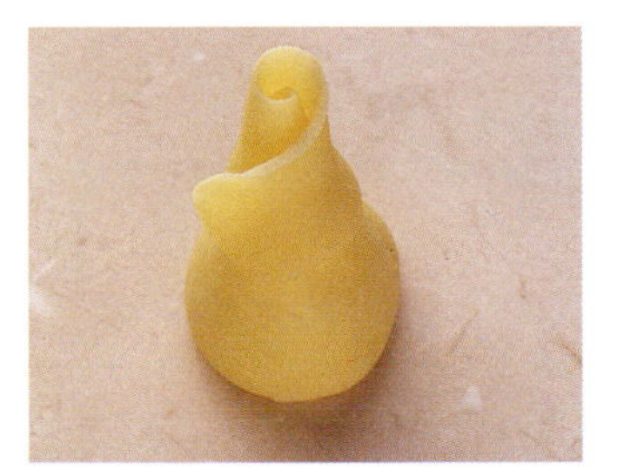

4. Wrap first petal around the point of the cone to form a bud.

5. Press three more petals around the base of the bud. Gently curl edges of petals.

6. Make five more petals using slightly larger balls of fondant. Flatten, then thin edge with finger and shape petals. Press petals under first row of petals. Continue, placing petals in between and slightly lower than previous row.

Fondant Leaves

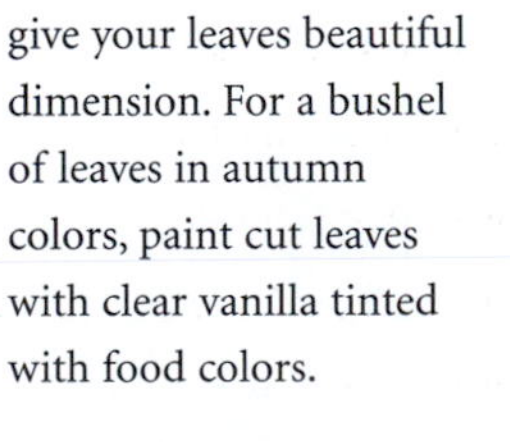

The veining tool helps give your leaves beautiful dimension. For a bushel of leaves in autumn colors, paint cut leaves with clear vanilla tinted with food colors.

1. Roll fondant to 1/8 inch thick.

2. Cut leaf shapes using Gum Paste Cutters.

3. Place leaves on a thin foam square. Use the veining tool to imprint veins. For a natural shape, dry in Flower Formers.

A WARM WELCOME

Instructions on page 102.

More to Know

We've saved some of the best finishing touches for last—learn about stenciling, adding painted color highlights and decorating with color flow. Also find important facts on storing, transporting and cutting your cake. And, when you're ready, use your decorating skills on all the cakes you've seen in this book—the complete decorating instructions are here.

Stenciling with Cake Sparkles™ on Icing

To keep excess Cake Sparkles from spilling out onto the cake top when you remove the stencil, spray the top of the stencil with non-stick cooking spray before stenciling. Loose Sparkles will stick on!

1. Ice cake and let icing crust slightly. Before starting, refer to directions on stencil package and spray stencil with non-stick cooking spray.

2. Position stencil on cake. Using a fine mesh strainer, sprinkle crushed Cake Sparkles carefully over stencil openings until filled in. Use the end of a wooden spoon to evenly push Cake Sparkles through strainer.

3. Remove stencil, placing spatula under one side and lifting off.

Stenciling with Buttercream on Fondant

Stenciling with icing is most easily accomplished using an angled spatula—it keeps your fingers out of the icing. Apply one color at a time and spread the icing completely over the area in the stencil for the best coverage.

1. Position stencil on cake. Use buttercream icing in a parchment bag with opening cut to the size of tip 3; fill in design with appropriate colors. Smooth with tapered spatula.

2. Carefully remove stencil, placing clean tapered spatula under one edge and lifting off edge of stencil.

3. Fill in any areas you missed with piped icing. Flatten and smooth with fingers dipped in cornstarch.

Stenciling Using Doily and Powdered Sugar on Chocolate Icing or Chocolate Cake

An intricate, pure white pattern against a chocolate background makes a fancy, but easy-to-do cake design. To guarantee success, use a double-thick doily, sift the confectioners' sugar and apply sugar heavily. Lift doily off carefully!

1. Ice cake and let icing crust about 30 minutes. Position doily on cake top.

2. Using a fine mesh strainer, sprinkle confectioners' sugar over doily openings until filled in.

3. Carefully remove doily.

Painting on Buttercream and Royal Icings

It's easy to add beautiful designs and color effects to buttercream cakes and royal icing flowers. Use a fine artist's brush to apply color.

1. Mix each icing color with a little clear vanilla extract for the perfect painting consistency. Test the color's intensity before painting by brushing it on a swatch of icing.

2. Transfer design pattern to your cake, then outline design with your brush. Or, pipe a freehand design if you wish.

3. Paint highlights, veins and edging on dried royal icing flowers. Let dry completely.

Decorating Cupcakes

Other quick ways with cupcakes—use a spatula to ice fluffy or dip cupcake top in melted fudge icing and twist; add sprinkles for extra fun! For a fancier look, try covering cupcakes using ruffle tip 124.

1. Use tip 1M. Hold tip at 90° angle to surface of cupcake. Pipe a spiral of icing, beginning at the outer edge and working inward. Stop pressure, pull tip away.

2. Pipe a second spiral on top.

3. End spiral by increasing pressure at center, stop pressure, pull tip away.

CUPCAKES WITH SPRINKLES

Why serve a plain cupcake when it takes just minutes to pipe a fancy iced top and add colorful sprinkles? Instructions above.

BOWS ALL AROUND

Elegant bows have an openwork look that works well with fresh flowers. Pipe bows in royal icing using the pattern on page 103 and the sotas technique. Instructions on page 102.

To test color flow for the right consistency, drop a dollop of color flow icing back into the mixture. When it takes a full count of ten for the icing to sink back into the mixture with the outline ring completely gone, the color flow icing is ready!

1. Trace your design pattern onto parchment paper, then tape tracing onto a cake circle (the back of a cookie pan makes a great work surface). Cover with waxed paper; smooth and tape. Using tip 2 and a parchment bag half-filled with full strength color flow, squeeze, pull and drop icing string following pattern outline. Stop, touch tip to surface and pull away. If you will be using the same color to fill in, let outline dry a few minutes until it "crusts." To prevent bleeding of colors, let outline dry 1-2 hours before filling in.
2. Thin down color flow mixture with water. Cut opening in parchment bag to the size of tip 2. Fill in design with thinned color flow.
3. Let decorations air dry thoroughly at least 48 hours. To remove, cut away waxed paper from board, then turn over and peel waxed paper off the color flow piece.

Royal Icing Lace Pieces

Carefully remove dried royal icing lace from its waxed paper backing with an angled spatula.

1. Trace lace pattern onto parchment paper, then tape onto cake board. Cover pattern with waxed paper. Using tip 1 and parchment bag, squeeze, pull and drop icing string to outline pattern.
2. Pipe center design and add tip 1 dots.
3. Add outside loops. Let dry for several hours. Carefully slide off waxed paper using a small angled spatula.

Chocolate Lace Pieces

To set chocolate lace, air dry or refrigerate for a short time. Never place in the freezer—waxed paper may buckle and distort your lace pieces.

1. Cover lace pattern with waxed paper. Melt Wilton Light Cocoa Candy Melts®; place in disposable decorating bag or parchment triangle fitted with tip 1 or 2. Squeeze out candy to outline pattern.
2. Continue piping pattern to complete design. Work quickly so Candy Melts stay fluid and easy to pipe. Keep your bag on a warming tray when not piping to keep fluid.
3. Add tip 1 or 2 dots. Refrigerate to set 5 minutes. Carefully slide off waxed paper using a small angled spatula.

Using Fresh Flowers on Cakes

The beauty and color of fresh flowers adds a special impact to cakes. A spray of petunias, a cascade of orchids or a single gardenia bloom looks lovely against a decorated cake background. Some flowers, such as violets, lavender, certain roses and nasturtiums are actually edible and can be positioned on a cake to impart a delicate flavor. Pretty herbs, such as marjoram and lemon balm that have flowered, can also be used.

No matter what flower you choose, and how you display it, certain precautions must be taken when using fresh flowers on cakes.

Many flowers are toxic or poisonous. Never place any flowers or greenery on or near food without first consulting your florist, botanical society or poison control center to be certain that it is safe. Be sure to specify what part of the plant you are using, as some parts of the plant may be safe to use, and others not. Stamens and styles found in a flower's center may cause an allergic reaction; consider removing them from the flowers before use. In addition, many purchased flowers are sprayed with pesticides. Ask for pesticide-free flowers, or use flowers you grow yourself.

Never put flowers directly on the cake; use separator plates, floral bowls, plastic wrap, waxed paper or doilies to keep the flowers from touching the cake. Never insert stems directly into the cake; use flower spikes.

Wilton has a variety of products to safely hold flowers for display on cakes, including crystal-look bowls, flower spikes, bases, rings, flower/candle holders and more. See the Wilton Yearbook of Cake Decorating or your Wilton dealer for the complete selection.

Using Flowers in a Crystal-look Bowl

Silk flowers arranged in a crystal-look bowl are a beautiful alternative to fresh and the arrangement becomes a lasting reminder of your spectacular cake. Assemble using floral foam designed for dry arrangements, and omit the water, of course!

1. Use water-absorbing foam for fresh flowers. Cut foam, soak in water and secure in bowl using waterproof floral tape.

2. Arrange flowers by pushing stems into foam.

3. Position bowl on cake.

Using Flowers in Flower Spikes

Flower Spikes are used for more than just flowers. Use them as a safe and clean way to add all types of other accents to cakes. Spikes can hold trims on wire stems such as doves and hearts, pearl sprays, curled ribbon, bows, tulle puffs, even balloons.

1. Insert Flower Spikes in cake. Be creative with your arrangements; spikes can be positioned on cake top or sides.

2. Using a small eyedropper, fill spike ¼ full of water. Be careful not to overfill or water will spill on cake when flowers are added.

3. Insert flower stems into spikes.

Party Cake Data & Cutting Guide
2 Inch High Pans (for 2-layer, 4 inch high cakes)

PAN SHAPE	SIZE	# SERVINGS	CUPS BATTER 1 LAYER, 2 IN.	BAKING TEMPERATURE	BAKING TIME MINUTES
Round	6"	8	2	350°	25-30
	8"	12	3	350°	30-35
	9"	22	5 1/2	350°	30-35
	10"	24	6	350°	35-40
	12"	30	7 1/2	350°	35-40
	14"	40	10	325°	50-55
	16"	60	15	325°	55-60
Sheet	7 x 11"	22	5 1/2	350°	30-35
	9 x 13"	28	7	350°	35-40
	11 x 15"	44	11	325°	35-40
	12 x 18"	56	14	325°	40-45
Square	6"	8	2	350°	25-30
	8"	16	4	350°	35-40
	10"	24	6	350°	35-40
	12"	40	10	350°	40-45
	14"	54	13 1/2	350°	45-50
	16"	62	15 1/2	350°	45-50
Heart	6"	6	1 1/2	350°	25-35
	9"	14	3 1/2	350°	30-35
	12"	32	8	350°	30-35
	15"	46	11 1/2	325°	40-45
Petal	6"	6	1 1/2	350°	25-30
	9"	14	3 1/2	350°	35-40
	12"	28	7	350°	35-40
	15"	48	12	325°	50-55
Hexagon	6"	7	1 3/4	350°	30-35
	9"	14	3 1/2	350°	35-40
	12"	24	6	350°	40-45
	15"	44	11	325°	40-45
Oval	7 3/4 x 5 5/8"	9	2 1/4	350°	25-30
	10 3/4 x 7 7/8"	20	5	350°	25-30
	13 x 9 7/8"	30	7 1/2	350°	25-30
	16 x 12 3/8"	44	11	325°	40-45

Party Cake Data & Cutting Guide
3 Inch High Pans (for 1-layer 3 inch high cakes, torted and filled)

PAN SHAPE	SIZE	# SERVINGS	CUPS BATTER 1 LAYER, 3 IN.	BAKING TEMPERATURE	BAKING TIME MINUTES
Round	6"	6	3	350°	35-40
	8"	10	5	350°	55-60
	10"	16	8	325°	65-75
	12"	22	11	325°	65-75
	14"	30	15	325°	80-85
	16"	36	18	325°	75-85
	18" Half (2 halves)	48	12	325°	60-65
Square	8"	13	6 1/2	350°	65-75
	10"	18	9	325°	65-75
	12"	28	14	325°	65-75
	14" (Use 2 cores)	38	19	350°	65-75
Sheet	9 x 13"	23	11 1/2	325°	60-75
	11 x 15"	32	16	325°	80-85
	12 x 18"	40	20	325°	85-90
Contour	7"	6	3	350°	45-50
	9"	11	5 1/2	350°	45-50
	11"	16	8	325°	80-85
	13"	22	11	325°	75-85
	15"	32	16	325°	75-80
Beveled	8 x 2"	6	3	350°	35-40
	10 x 2"	10	5	350°	35-40
	12 x 2"	14	7	350°	45-50
	14 x 1 1/4"	12	6	325°	45-50
	16 x 1 1/4"	16	8	325°	45-50

NOTE: FOR PANS 10" AND LARGER, USE A HEATING CORE WHEN BAKING.

It's important to know approximately how many servings your decorated cake will yield. That's why we have provided an estimated number of servings for each cake design in this book. It also helps to have a plan when you are cutting the cake. This will help you serve attractive, uniform pieces while reaching your targeted number of servings.

The charts at left show baking information and serving amounts for both 2 inch high and 3 inch high pans. The figures for 2 inch high pans are based on a 2-layer or 4 inch high cake. The figures for 3 inch high pans are based on a 1-layer cake which has been torted and filled to reach a 3 inch height.

The serving amounts listed are based on party-sized portions of approximately 1 1/2 x 2 inches (wedding-sized portions are cut smaller). You may wish to cut larger or smaller pieces, depending on whether you are using a 4 inch layer or a 3 inch layer. **The number of servings given is meant as a guide only. In general, each 1/2 cup of batter equals 1 serving.**

CUTTING GUIDES

The diagrams shown represent the cutting plan for specific pan shapes. You will use the same general technique to cut each size cake in that shape.

Rounds

To cut round cakes, move in two inches from the cake's outer edge; cut a circle and then slice approximately 1 1/2 inch pieces within the circle. Now move in another 2 inches, cut another circle, slice approximately 1 1/2 inch pieces and so on until the cake is completely cut. *Note: 6 inch diameter cakes should be cut in wedges, without a center circle.*

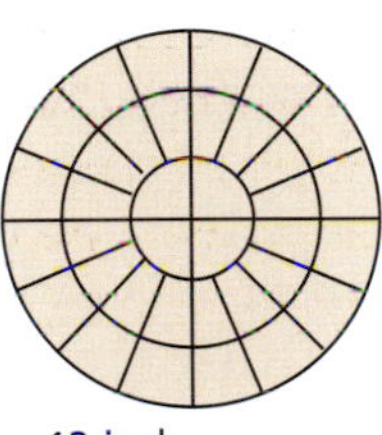

12 inch

Cut Petal, Hexagon, Beveled and Contour cakes similar to round tiers.

Squares

To cut square cakes, move in 2 inches from the outer edge and cut across. Then slice approximately 1 1/2 inch pieces of cake. Now move in another 2 inches and slice again until the entire cake is cut.

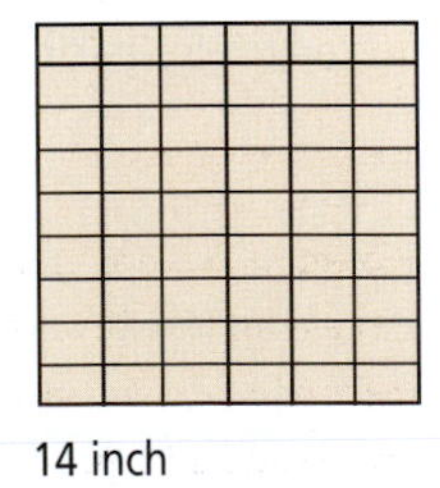

14 inch

Sheets

Cut sheet cakes similar to square cakes.

11 x 15 inch

Hearts

To cut heart-shaped cakes, divide vertically into halves, quarters, sixths or eighths depending on cake diameter. Within rows, slice approximately 1 1/2 inch pieces of cake.

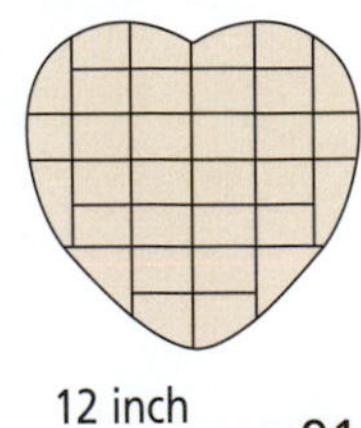

12 inch

Icing Recipes

Buttercream Icing

1/2 cup solid vegetable shortening

1/2 cup butter or margarine*

1 teaspoon Wilton Clear Vanilla Extract**

4 cups (approx. 1 lb.) sifted confectioners' sugar

2 tablespoons milk

YIELD: 3 cups

Cream butter and shortening with electric mixer. Add vanilla. Gradually add sugar, one cup at a time, beating well on medium speed. Scrape sides and bottom of bowl often. When all sugar has been mixed in, icing will appear dry. Add milk and beat at medium speed until light and fluffy. Keep icing covered with a damp cloth until ready to use. Refrigerate leftover icing in an airtight container, up to 2 weeks. Rewhip before using.

* *For pure white icing and stiffer consistency, substitute all-vegetable shortening and 1/2 teaspoon Wilton Butter Extract for butter/margarine. Margarine may give icing a softer texture than butter, and is less desirable for decorating.*

** *To vary flavor and add some fun, substitute Wilton Candy Flavors for Vanilla Extract.*

Chocolate Buttercream Icing

Add to above recipe:

3/4 cup cocoa powder for baking or 3 1-oz. unsweetened chocolate squares for baking, melted

Additional 1-2 tablespoons milk*

YIELD: 3 cups

Mix until well blended.

* *For Chocolate Mocha Icing, substitute freshly brewed strong coffee for additional milk.*

Time Saver Tip

Creamy White Icing Mix

Just add butter and milk (and any color) for a rich, homemade buttercream taste. YIELD: 2 cups.

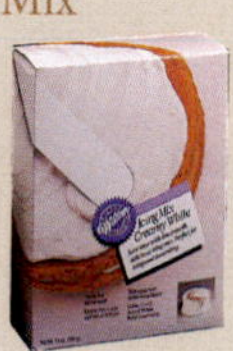

Snow-White Buttercream Icing

2/3 cup water

4 tablespoons Wilton Meringue Powder

12 cups (approx. 3 lbs.) sifted confectioners' sugar

1 1/4 cups solid shortening

3/4 teaspoon salt

1/2 teaspoon Wilton Almond Extract

1/2 teaspoon Wilton Clear Vanilla Extract

1/4 teaspoon Wilton Butter Flavor

YIELD: 7 cups

Recipe may be doubled or halved. If halved, yield is 2 2/3 cups.

Combine water and Meringue Powder. Whip at high speed until peaks form. Add 4 cups sugar, one cup at a time, beating after each addition at low speed. Alternately add shortening and remainder of sugar. Add salt and flavorings. Beat at low speed until smooth.

Time Saver Tip

Wilton Ready-To-Use Decorator Icing

The ideal consistency for decorating and icing. Just stir and use; pure white is easy to color, too. 16 oz. cans, available in White and Chocolate. Hint: to make black icing that is ideal for decorating and tastes good, too, begin with Chocolate Ready-To-Use Decorator Icing and add black icing color.

Royal Icing

3 level tablespoons Wilton Meringue Powder

4 cups (approx. 1 lb.) sifted confectioners' sugar

6 tablespoons water*

YIELD: 3 cups

Beat all ingredients at low speed for 7-10 minutes (10-12 minutes at high speed for portable mixer) until icing forms peaks.

* *When using large countertop mixer or for stiffer icing, use 1 tablespoon less water.*

Fluffy Boiled Icing

Meringue:

3 tablespoons Wilton Meringue Powder

1/2 cup cold water

Syrup:

2 cups granulated sugar

1/4 cup corn syrup

1/2 cup water

YIELD: 8 cups

Beat meringue powder and cold water until stiff, about 4 minutes. In large microwave-safe measuring cup, stir sugar, corn syrup and water. In microwave oven*, bring syrup mixture to a boil (approximately 5 minutes). Remove when boiling stops. Slowly add syrup to meringue mixture while beating on low speed. Beat on high speed for 4 minutes until stiff and glossy.

* *For top of range, mix sugar, corn syrup and water in 2 quart saucepan. Bring to a boil, cool slightly and follow directions above.*

Stabilized Whipped Cream Icing

1 cup heavy whipping cream (1/2 pint)

2 tablespoons confectioners' sugar

2 tablespoons Wilton Piping Gel

1/2 teaspoon Wilton Clear Vanilla

YIELD: 1 1/2 to 2 cups

Combine whipping cream and sugar in mixing bowl. Whip to soft peak stage. Add piping gel and vanilla, then continue to whip stiff peaks. Do not overbeat.

Time Saver Tip

Wilton Whipped Icing Mix

Just add ice water to this Wilton exclusive, and whip up velvety-smooth icing with a perfect consistency for icing cakes and piping decorations. YIELD: 4 cups.

Rolled Fondant

1 tablespoon unflavored gelatin

1/4 cup cold water

1/2 cup Wilton Glucose

1 tablespoon Wilton Glycerin

2 tablespoons solid vegetable shortening

8 cups (approx. 2 lbs.) sifted confectioners' sugar

2-3 drops of desired liquid food color and flavoring

Cornstarch and extra confectioners' sugar (to dust surface for rolling)

Apricot glaze and/or buttercream icing to coat cake surface*

YIELD: Covers a 10 x 4 inch high cake

Note: Prior to applying the fondant, the cake must be prepared with an undercoating of apricot glaze and/or a light layer of buttercream icing. The undercoating is used to enhance the flavor, seal in moisture, ease application of the fondant and adhere it to the cake.

Combine gelatin and cold water. Let stand until thick. Place gelatin mixture in top of double boiler and heat until dissolved. Add glucose and glycerin; mix well. Stir in shortening, and just before it is completely melted, remove from heat, add flavoring and color. Mixture should cool until lukewarm. Next, place 4 cups of the sifted confectioners' sugar in a bowl and make a well. Pour the lukewarm gelatin mixture into the well and stir with a wooden spoon, mixing in sugar and adding more, a little at a time, until stickiness disappears. Knead in remaining sugar. Continue kneading until the fondant is smooth, pliable and does not stick to your hands. If fondant is too soft, add more sugar; if too stiff, add water (a drop at a time). Use fondant immediately or store in an airtight container in refrigerator. When ready to use, bring to room temperature and knead again until soft.

To roll fondant, first spray work surface and rolling pin with vegetable oil pan spray and dust with a mixture of confectioners' sugar and cornstarch. Prepare the cake by applying the buttercream or apricot glaze. Roll out fondant into a circle the diameter of the cake plus double the height of the cake. As you roll, lift and move the fondant to prevent it from sticking to the surface. Gently lift fondant over rolling pin and place over cake. Smooth and shape fondant on cake using the Wilton Easy Glide Fondant Smoother. If large air bubbles are trapped under fondant, prick with a pin and continue to smooth. Trim excess from base with a knife.

Time Saver Tip

Wilton Ready-To-Use Fondant

Available in White (add any color) and Chocolate, Wilton Ready-to-Use Fondant requires no mixing and comes with easy-to-follow directions. Just roll, apply and shape. A 24 oz. package covers an 8 inch two-layer cake plus decorations.

Quick-Pour Fondant

6 cups (approx. 1 1/2 lbs.) confectioners' sugar, sifted

1/2 cup (4 oz.) water

2 tablespoons white corn syrup

1 teaspoon Wilton Almond Extract

Desired Wilton Icing Color (optional)

Apricot glaze and/or buttercream icing to coat cake surface

YIELD: 4 cups, enough to cover a 10-inch round cake.

Recipe may be doubled or tripled.

Combine water and corn syrup. Add to sugar in a saucepan and stir over low heat until well-mixed and heated to 92° F., thin enough to be poured, but thick enough so it will not run off the cake. If fondant mixture is heated too high, it will lose its shine on the cake.

Stir in extract and icing color, if desired. Prepare the cake by applying the buttercream or apricot glaze. Place cake on cooling rack with a cookie sheet beneath it. Pour fondant over prepared cake, flowing from center and moving out in a circular motion. Touch up sides with a spatula.

Chocolate-Poured Fondant

Add to Quick-Pour Fondant recipe:

1 oz. water

3 oz. melted, unsweetened chocolate

YIELD: 4 cups, enough to cover a 10 inch round cake.

Recipe may be doubled or tripled.

Follow Quick-Pour Fondant recipe, but after fondant is heated, stir in melted chocolate, then add flavoring.

Apricot Glaze

1 cup apricot preserves

YIELD: Covers a 10 x 4 inch cake.

Ideal for preparing a cake for fondant application or crumb-coating cakes before icing.

Heat apricot preserves to boiling, strain. Brush on cake while still hot. Let dry. Glaze will dry to a hard finish in 15 minutes or less.

Cream Cheese Icing

1/2 cup (1 stick) butter

8 oz. package cream cheese, softened

4 cups (approx. 1 lb.) confectioners' sugar

1 tablespoon milk

YIELD: 2 3/4 cups

For best results, do not use light cream cheese or a butter substitute. If margarine is used, icing will be softer.

In a medium mixing bowl, cream butter and cream cheese until smooth, add sugar and milk. Beat on high speed until smooth (30-60 seconds). Use this thicker consistency for piping borders. For icing cakes smooth, thin with milk.

Icing Chart

ICING TYPE	FLAVOR/ DESCRIPTION	CONSISTENCY	BEST USED FOR...	COLORING	STORAGE/ FRESHNESS	SPECIAL INFORMATION
Buttercream (Wilton Mix or Homemade)	Sweet, buttery flavor Tastes the best and looks beautiful for most decorating	Thin-to-stiff consistency depending on the amount of corn syrup or sugar added (sugar stiffens)	Icing cakes smooth Borders, writing Most decorations including roses, drop flowers, sweet peas and figure piping	Yields all colors Most colors deepen upon setting. Let icing set 2-3 hours for deep color Some colors may fade upon sitting in bright light	Icing can be refrigerated in airtight container for 2 weeks	Iced cake can be stored at room temperature for 2-3 days Flowers remain soft enough to be cut with a knife
Snow-White Buttercream (Homemade)	Sweet, almond flavor Ideal for wedding cakes Icing cakes smooth	Thin-to-stiff consistency depending on the amount of corn syrup or sugar added (sugar stiffens)	Borders, writing, flowers Most decorations	Yields truer colors due to pure white base color Creates deep colors Most colors deepen upon setting	Icing can be refrigerated in airtight container for 2 weeks Iced cake can be stored at room temperature for 2-3 days	Air-dried flowers have translucent look Flowers remain soft enough to be cut with a knife
Wilton Decorator White (Ready-to-Use)	Sweet, vanilla flavor Convenient, ready-to-spread icing Pure white color is ideal for coloring	Ready-to-use Can make roses right from the can	Shells, stars, flowers-use from container Roses - may stiffen with confectioners' sugar Icing cakes, writing, leaves - thin with milk, water or corn syrup	Yields truer colors due to pure white base color Creates deep colors Most colors deepen upon setting	Leftover icing can be refrigerated for 2 weeks Iced cake can be stored at room temperature for 2-3 days	Available for purchase through Wilton Yearbook or any authorized Wilton retailer
Wilton Decorator Chocolate (Ready-to-use)	Sweet chocolate flavor Convenient ready-to-spread icing	Ready-to-use Can make roses right from the can	Shells, stars, flowers—use from container Roses—may stiffen with confectioners' sugar Icing cakes, writing, leaves, thin with milk, water or corn syrup	Recommended when black icing is needed. Add a little black icing color to chocolate for a better tasting black icing. Use when brown icing is directed.	Leftover icing can be refrigerated for 2 weeks. Iced cake can be stored at room temperature for 2-3 days.	Available for purchase through Wilton Yearbook or any authorized Wilton retailer.
Royal (Made with Wilton Meringue Powder)	Very sweet flavor Dries candy-hard for lasting decorations	Thin-to-stiff consistency depending on the amount of water added	Flower-making, figure piping, making flowers on wires Decorating cookies and gingerbread houses	Yields deep colors Some colors may fade upon sitting in bright light Requires more base color than buttercream to achieve the same intensity	Icing can be stored in airtight, grease-free container at room temperature for 2 weeks Air-dried decorations last for months	Bowls/utensils must be grease-free Cover icing with damp cloth to prevent crusting
Rolled Fondant (Wilton Ready-to-Use White or Chocolate Homemade Rolled Fondant)	Rich, sweet flavor Covers cakes with a perfectly smooth, satiny iced surface Easy and fast to use Knead in flavor of your choice	Dough-like consistency that is rolled out before cake application Stays semi-soft on cakes	Any firm pound or fruit cake Cutting, molding and modeling decorations	Yields pastels to deep colors	Excess can be stored 2 months in an airtight container Iced cake can be stored at room temperature for 3-4 days	Prior to applying fondant, cake must be covered in apricot glaze and/or buttercream icing, seals in freshness and moisture
Quick-Pour Fondant (Homemade)	Very sweet flavor Covers cakes with a perfectly smooth, shiny iced surface Coats baked goods and seals in freshness with a shiny, smooth surface	Pours and dries to a semi-hard, smooth surface	All cakes, petit fours and cookies	Yields pastels	Use immediately Excess fondant may be refrigerated, reheated and poured again	Prior to applying fondant, cake must be covered in apricot glaze and/or buttercream icing, seals in freshness and moisture
Whipped Icing Mix (Wilton Mix)	Light, delicate taste in Vanilla and Chocolate flavors Holds shape like no other mix Easy to make	Perfect, velvety consistency for decorating everything from stars, roses and borders to garlands and writing	Icing cakes Most decorations Toppings on pies, puddings, tarts and more	Vanilla yields any color	Icing can be refrigerated in airtight container. Iced cake can be stored at room temperature for 2-3 days	Exclusive Wilton formula Available for purchase through Wilton Yearbook or any authorized Wilton retailer
Fluffy Boiled Icing (Homemade)	Marshmallow-like flavor 100% fat-free	Very fluffy consistency Sets quickly	Icing cakes smooth and fluffy Borders, figure piping, writing, stringwork	Yields pastels and deep colors	Use immediately	Iced cake can be stored at room temperature Serve within 24 hours
Stabilized Whipped Cream (Homemade)	Creamy, delicate sweetness	Light, thin-to-medium consistency	All cakes but especially those decorated with fruits Borders, large tip work, writing	Yields pastels only	Use immediately	Iced cake must be refrigerated Texture remains soft on decorated cake

Transporting Cakes

Transporting a cake, especially a long distance, can be a challenge. Follow these guidelines to assure your cake arrives at its destination in perfect condition.

Be sure your cake is on a sturdy base. Cakes on pillars must be transported unassembled. toppers, candles, and ornaments should not be placed on cake. Place your cake in a clean, covered box that is sized to the base. This will prevent the cake from shifting within the box and possibly crushing the sides of the cake. If you find that your box is too big, remove cake, roll pieces of masking tape, sticky side out, and attach to the inside bottom of box. Position the cake base on top of tape. The tape will hold the base in place within the box. Place the box on carpet foam or a non-skid mat on the floor of the car. Keep the box flat, do not place on car seat. Cake can also be transported in the trunk of the car if the weather is cool. Drive carefully! To remove cake, cut side of box.

Bring along extra icing, tips, spatula and flowers in case you need to repair any damage at your destination.

Storing Your Cake

Take some final precautions and store your cake the best way possible. After all, your time, effort and creativity have made it very special!

Beware of the following factors, which can affect the look of your decorated cake:

Sunlight — will alter icing colors. Keep your cake stored in a covered box and out of direct sunlight.

Humidity — can soften royal icing and gum paste decorations. If you live in a climate with high humidity, prepare your royal icing using only pure cane confectioners' sugar (not dextrose or beet sugar), add less liquid and add 1 teaspoon more Meringue Powder to the recipe.

Heat — can melt icing and cause decorations to droop. Keep your decorated cake as cool as possible and stabilize your buttercream icing by adding 2 teaspoons Meringue Powder per recipe.

Protect your cake by placing it in a clean, covered cake box. Avoid using foil or plastic wrap to cover a decorated cake — these materials can stick to icing and crush delicate decorations.

The icing that covers your cake determines how it should be stored — in the refrigerator, or at cool room temperature, or frozen, if storing for longer than 3 days. If you want to store your iced cake in a different way than noted, make a small test cake.

Buttercream Icing — cakes iced with these icings can be stored at room temperature or refrigerated for 2-3 days. Cake can be frozen.

Fluffy Boiled Icing — can be stored at room temperature, best if served within 24 hours. Do not freeze.

Stabilized Whipped Cream — cake must be refrigerated immediately after decorating.

Rolled Fondant Icing — cakes covered with rolled fondant icing can be stored at room temperature 3 to 4 days. Do not refrigerate or freeze, condensation will form on fondant.

Quick-Pour Fondant Icing — it coats cakes, petit fours and cookies while sealing in freshness. Items can be stored at room temperature for 3 to 4 days.

Wilton Decorator Icings — Cakes iced with these icings can be stored at room temperature or refrigerated for 2-3 days. Cake can be frozen.

Wilton Whipped Icing Mix — Iced cakes can be stored at room temperature or refrigerated for 2-3 days.

Royal Icing — cakes decorated with thoroughly-dried royal icing decorations should be stored according to the type of icing they are covered with. However, if royal icing decorations are to be put on a cake that will be frozen, it is recommended that icing decorations be placed on the cakes after thawing, so that colored decorations won't bleed from condensation.

Brimming With Roses

as seen on the Cover and Page 59

Techniques Needed

Roses, Balls, Beads, Leaves

Wilton Checklist

Pan: 8 x 3 inch Round
Tips: 2, 5, 12, 104, 352
Colors: Garden Tone Icing Colors: Aster Mauve, Juniper Green; Pink
Other: Flower Nail No. 9, Meringue Powder Mix, Decorator Favorites Pattern Press Set (vine press used), Cake Circle, waxed paper, cornstarch

Ingredients List

Cake: Prepared 1-Layer Round (torted and filled to 3 inches high)
Icing Recipes: Royal, Buttercream Icings (2 recipes each)

Tint royal icing a combination of aster mauve and pink; make half dark aster mauve/pink combination and half light aster mauve/pink combination. Using the flower nail, make 20 dark aster mauve/pink and 20 lt. aster mauve/pink tip 104 roses with tip 12 bases. Make extras to allow for breakage and let dry for 1-2 days.

Ice cake smooth in lt. aster mauve/pink buttercream icing; let icing set approximately 15 minutes. Lightly dust vine pattern press with cornstarch and randomly imprint design on cake sides. Using lt. aster mauve/pink buttercream icing, pipe tip 2 balls on imprinted areas; add tip 5 bead bottom border.

Using tip 12 and lt. aster mauve/pink buttercream icing, pipe mounds of icing at varying heights on cake top and position roses. Pipe tip 352 leaves using juniper green buttercream icing. Serves 10.

Spring Flower Basket

as seen on Pages 6 & 47

Techniques Needed

Daisies, Drop Flowers, Basketweave, Writing

Wilton Checklist

Pan: 9 x 2 inch Heart
Tips: 2, 3, 47, 103, 104, 131, 225
Colors: Delphinium Blue, Buttercup Yellow
Other: Flower Nail #7, Cake Board, Fanci-Foil Wrap, Meringue Powder, Flower Former Set, waxed paper, granulated sugar

Ingredients List

Cake: Prepared 2-Layer Heart 3 inches high
Icing Recipes: Buttercream Icing (2 recipes), Royal Icing (1 recipe)

In advance, using royal icing, make 5 tip 104 white daisies and 10 tip 103 white daisies, all with tip 3 yellow centers. Dust centers with granulated sugar. Make 110 tip 225 blue drop flowers and 40 tip 131 blue drop flowers all with tip 3 yellow centers. Make extras of all to allow for breakage and let dry (dry daisies on medium flower former).

Using buttercream icing, smooth ice top in white and sides in delphinium blue. Pipe tip 47 basketweave in delphinium blue on cake sides. Pipe tip 47 rope bottom border in blue. Write tip 2 blue name. Attach flowers to top edge with Buttercream Icing. Serves 10.

Happiest Clown in Town!

as seen on Page 12

Techniques Needed

Drop Flowers, Drop Strings, Shells, Zigzag Garland, Rosettes, Balloons (figure piping)

Wilton Checklist

Pan: 8 x 2 inch Round
Tips: 2, 3, 12, 16, 18, 224
Colors: Leaf Green, Royal Blue, Christmas Red, Golden Yellow
Other: Clown 'n Around Topper, Rainbow Wavy Sparkler Candles, Meringue Powder, Cake Dividing Set, Cake Circle, waxed paper

Ingredients List

Cake: Prepared 2-Layer Round
Icing Recipes: Buttercream Icing (2 recipes), Royal Icing (1 recipe)

At least one day in advance, use royal icing and tip 224 to make 45 drop flowers (15 red, 15 blue, 15 green) with tip 2 yellow dot centers. Let dry.

Make balloons at least one day in advance: Using royal icing and tip 12, on waxed paper, figure pipe 8 each of green, red and blue with tip 3 ties. Let dry.

Spatula ice 2-layer cake smooth with yellow buttercream icing. Use Cake Dividing Set to divide cake into 8ths at top and bottom edges. Beginning at back of cake, pipe tip 3 triple drop strings from each division point, lowest string measuring $1\frac{1}{2}$ inches deep, middle string 1 inch deep and top string $\frac{1}{2}$ inch deep. Pipe tip 16 shell top border in yellow. Pipe tip 18 shell bottom border in yellow. Overpipe bottom shells with tip 18 zigzag garland. Add tip 3 double drop strings in yellow. Pipe tip 18 rosettes for candle holders. Position balloons, adding 3 strings. Position flowers, candles and topper. Serves 12.

NOTE: Just for Dad, shown page 12, is decorated with the same tips and techniques as Happiest Clown in Town, except for the following: Pipe tip 21 fleur de lis at garland points. Write tip 3 name. Eliminate balloons, rosettes, candles and topper. Use chocolate buttercream icing (no royal icing needed.)

Swept Up In Romance

as seen on Pages 12, 20 & 38

Techniques Needed

Drop Flowers, Zigzag Garland, Drop Strings, Shells

Wilton Checklist

Pan: 8 x 2 inch Round
Tips: 2, 3, 16, 18, 224
Ornament: Threshold of Happiness
Other: Cake Dividing Set, Meringue Powder, Cake Circle, waxed paper

Ingredients List

Cake: Prepared 2-Layer Round
Icing Recipes: Buttercream Icing (2 recipes), Royal Icing (1 recipe)

In advance, using royal icing on waxed paper covered board, make approximately 45 tip 224 drop flowers with tip 2 dot centers. Make extras to allow for breakage and let dry.

Ice the top and sides of 2-layer cake smooth with a spatula. Using cake dividing set, divide cake into 8ths at top and bottom, marking 1 inch from bottom up.

Pipe tip 3 triple drop string garlands from top division marks of cake; the bottom drop string should measure $1\frac{1}{2}$ inch deep, the middle $1\frac{1}{4}$ inch deep and the top 1 inch deep.

Pipe a tip 16 top shell border. Pipe a tip 18 bottom shell border. Pipe tip 18 zigzag garland starting at bottom division marks. Overpipe the garland with tip 3 double drop strings.

Position drop flowers on top of cake and at garland points. Position ornament. Serves 12.

NOTE: Spray of Daisies, shown page 12, is decorated with the same tips and techniques as Swept Up In Romance. Combine Aster Mauve and Rose Icing Colors to achieve shade shown. Eliminate ornament; position fresh flowers in Crystal-Look Bowl.

Celebration of Stars

as seen on Page 25

Techniques Needed

Stars

Wilton Checklist

Pan: 8 x 2 inch Round
Tips: 1G, 13, 131
Colors: Buttercup Yellow, Ivory
Other: Flower Spikes, Cake Circle, fresh flowers

Note: Combine icing colors to produce icing shade shown

Ingredients List

Cake: Prepared 2-Layer Round, (3 inches high)
Icing Recipes: Buttercream Icing ($1\frac{1}{2}$ recipes)

Ice 2-layer cake top and sides smooth in buttercream icing. Using tip 13, pipe stars on cake top and sides. Add tip 131 star top border and tip 1G star bottom border.

Insert a flower spike in center of cake and arrange fresh flowers. Serves 10.

Cascading Clusters

as seen on Page 26

Techniques Needed

Drop Flowers Dots

Wilton Checklist

Pan: 8 x 2 inch Square
Tips: 2, 3, 24, 129
Colors: Aster Mauve, Ivory
Other: Cake Board, Large Angled Spatula, Whipped Icing Mix, waxed paper

Ingredients List

Cake: Prepared 2-Layer Square
Icing Recipes: Royal Icing (1 recipe)

At least 1 day ahead of time, using royal icing on waxed paper covered board, make 140 tip 24 light mauve small drop flowers with tip 2 dark mauve dot centers and 150 tip 129 light mauve large drop flowers with tip 3 dark mauve dot centers. Let dry.

Add a small amount of ivory icing color to whipped icing. Ice top and sides of 2-layer cake fluffy with large angled spatula. Position clusters of flowers. Serves 16.

Fleur de Lis Fantasy

as seen on Page 29

Techniques Needed

Fleur-de-lis Shells

Wilton Checklist

Pan: 8 x 2 inch Round
Tips: 18, 32
Other: Cake Board, Fanci-Foil Wrap, Cake Dividing Set, sliced almonds

Ingredients List

Cake: Prepared 2-Layer Round
Icing Recipes: Chocolate Buttercream Icing

Ice top and sides of 2-layer cake smooth with chocolate buttercream icing. Sprinkle top of cake with sliced almonds. Use Cake Dividing Set to divide cake into 8ths, marking $1\frac{1}{2}$ inches below top cake edge. Pipe tip 32 fleur-de-lis at each division point. Pipe tip 18 top and tip 32 bottom shell borders with chocolate buttercream icing. Serves 12.

Years to Cherish

as seen on Page 31

Techniques Needed

Drop Flowers Rosettes
Writing E-motion

Wilton Checklist

Pan: 9 x 2 inch Heart
Tips: 2, 18, 32, 225
Colors: Aster Mauve, Delphinium Blue, Violet, Ivory
Other: Script Message Press Set, Cake Board, waxed paper

Ingredients List

Cake: Prepared 2-Layer Heart (3 inches high)
Icing Recipes: Buttercream Icing (2 recipes), Royal Icing (1 recipe)

Tint royal icing, $\frac{1}{3}$ Aster Mauve, $\frac{1}{3}$ Violet with a little Ivory, $\frac{1}{3}$ Delphinium Blue.

At least one day in advance, using royal icing on waxed paper covered board, make 45 tip 225 drop flowers (15 each: Aster Mauve, Violet, Delphinium Blue) with tip 2 white dot centers. Let dry.

Bake a 9 inch heart cake in two $1\frac{1}{2}$ inch deep layers, to measure 3 inches high. Using buttercream, ice sides and top of heart cake smooth with spatula. Pipe tip 18 rosettes around top edge of cake; position drop flower in each rosette, alternating colors.

Imprint message on cake top with press set; use tip 2 to write message. Pipe 3 tip 18 rosettes below message and position a drop flower on top of each.

Approximately $\frac{1}{2}$ inch from top rosette border, pipe tip 2 e-motion heart outline.

Add tip 32 bottom rosette border. Serves 10.

Scroll Enchantment

as seen on Page 32

Techniques Needed

Scrolls | Petunias

Wilton Checklist

Pan: 8 x 2 inch Round
Tips: 16, 103, 352
Colors: Leaf Green, Moss Green, Buttercup Yellow
Other: Cake Board, Decorator Favorites Pattern Press Set, Lily Nail Set, White Stamens, Cake Dividing Set, Meringue Powder, 3-inch aluminum foil squares

Ingredients List

Cake: Prepared 2-Layer Round
Icing Recipes: Buttercream Icing ($1\frac{1}{2}$ recipes), Royal Icing (1 recipe)

At least 48 hours in advance: Using tips 16 and 103 and white royal icing, make 20 petunias on foil-lined $1\frac{5}{8}$ inch lily nail. Insert 5 stamens in each petunia. Let flower completely dry before removing from foil.

Spatula ice 2-layer cake smooth with combination of Leaf Green, Moss Green and Buttercup Yellow buttercream icing. Use Cake Dividing Set to divide top of cake into 12ths. Imprint medium scroll from Pattern Press Set at each division point on cake top. Use small scroll to imprint 6 circular designs in center of cake top. On cake sides, imprint a continuous row of medium scrolls at top edge; imprint row of small scrolls centered between medium scrolls. Use tip 16 and white buttercream icing to pipe in all imprinted designs.

Position flowers and add tip 352 leaves in a combination of Moss Green and Buttercup Yellow buttercream. Serves 12.

The Bride's Entrance

as seen on Page 35

Techniques Needed

Sotas | Drop Flowers
Dots | Ruffles
Ruffle Garland | Leaves

Wilton Checklist

Pan: Wonder Mold
Tips: 1, 2, 102, 124, 131, 225, 349
Colors: Moss Green, Aster Mauve
Other: Teen Doll Pick, Cake Board, Decorator Brush Set, Meringue Powder, pink $\frac{1}{4}$ inch ribbon, 6 inch white tulle circle, styrofoam craft cube

Ingredients List

Cake: Prepared Wonder Mold
Icing Recipes: Royal Icing (1 recipe), Buttercream Icing (3 recipes)

At least one day in advance, make the following royal icing drop flowers: 10 tip 225 in white with tip 2 white dot centers; 10 tip 131 in mauve with tip 2 white dot centers. Let dry.

Using decorator brush and thinned down white buttercream icing, "paint" bodice area of doll pick that will be covered with dress. Position in styrofoam craft cube to dry.

Use spatula to heavily ice bottom of wonder mold cake with white buttercream icing. Form "pleats" on dress with spatula. Insert doll pick into dress. Using white buttercream icing, pipe tip 1 sotas to cover bodice and waist front and back area. Pipe tip 102 white buttercream ruffles around bottom edge of bodice.

Using tip 124 and white buttercream icing, pipe three rows of ruffles starting at bottom of dress and working upward. Add tip 102 ruffle garland above top ruffle. Pipe tip 1 dots on dress to resemble lace: pipe a center dot and add 6 smaller dots around center. Fold tulle in half and position on head with tip 2 dots of royal icing. Attach white drop flowers to top of veil with tip 2 dots of royal icing.

Attach flowers to hand with tip 2 dots of royal icing. Form into a bouquet, add tip 349 leaves and attach ribbon. Serves 12.

Garden Garlands

as seen on Page 37

Techniques Needed

Triple Swag Garland | Balls

Wilton Checklist

Pan: 7 x 2 inch Round
Tips: 5, 124
Color: Buttercup Yellow
Other: Flower Spikes, Cake Dividing Set, Cake Board, Fanci-Foil Wrap, fresh flowers

Ingredients List

Cake: Prepared 2-Layer Round
Icing Recipes: Buttercream Icing (1 recipe)

Tint icing yellow. Ice 2-layer cake smooth with spatula.

Using Cake Dividing Set, divide cake into 6 sections.

Use tip 124 to pipe triple swag garland from each of the 6 division points. (Note: Pipe the deepest swag first. Lowest swag is $1\frac{1}{4}$ inches deep; middle is 1 inch deep; top is $\frac{3}{4}$ inch deep) Pipe tip 5 ball top and bottom borders. Pipe tip 5 balls on center of cake top. Position fresh flowers in flower spikes and insert in cake. Serves 10.

Dinnertime at the Zoo!

as seen on Page 42

Techniques Needed

Figure Piping | Zigzags

Wilton Checklist

Pan: Standard Muffin
Tips: 1, 1A, 2, 2A, 3, 5, 6, 12, 13, 67, 81, 349
Colors: Kelly Green, Black, Pink, Lemon Yellow, Orange
Other: White Standard Baking Cups, 4 inch Lollipop Sticks, 3 x $2\frac{1}{2}$ inch white construction paper

Ingredients List

Cake: Prepared Cupcakes
Icing Recipe: Buttercream Icing (1 recipe), Royal Icing (optional)

Ice cupcakes smooth with green buttercream icing.

(Note: Animal figures can be piped directly on cupcakes in buttercream or can be made ahead of time in royal icing and set aside to dry for later positioning on cupcakes.)

To Make Lamb: Use white icing and tip 1A to pipe elongated body and ball head.

Insert tip 5 in sides of body and slowly pull out to pipe legs. Pipe tip 5 muzzle on head and add tip 81 pull-out ears. Cover body with tip 13 zigzag fur. Pipe tip 3 black hooves, tip 1 black dot eyes and tip 1 pink dot nose.

To Make Chick: Use tip 2A and yellow icing to pipe body and ball head. Add tip 67 yellow pull-out wings and tip 349 feathers on head. Pipe-in tip 2 orange feet and pull-out beak. Add tip 1 white dot eyes and tip 1 black dot pupils.

To Make Pig: Use tip 2A and pink icing to pipe elongated body. Pipe tip 12 ball head and pull-out legs. Add tip 6 snout. Pipe tip 2 black dot eyes and swirl motion curly tail. Add tip 81 pull-out ears.

Print message on sign with marker and tape to lollipop stick. Insert into cupcakes. Each serves 1.

Fancy Fruitcake

as seen on Page 44

Techniques Needed

Figure Piping, Lattice, Shell-Motion, Dots, Leaves

Wilton Checklist

Pan: 7 x 2 inch Round
Tips: 2, 3, 5, 47, 349
Colors: Ivory, Buttercup Yellow, Christmas Red, Violet, Brown, Leaf Green, Golden Yellow, Lemon Yellow
Other: Cake Board, Fanci-Foil Wrap, Meringue Powder

Ingredients List

Cake: Prepared 2-Layer Round, (3 inches high)
Icing Recipes: Buttercream Icing ($1^1/_2$ recipes), Royal Icing (1 recipe)

In advance, using royal icing and figure piping instructions (page 43), pipe cherries, grapes and bananas. Set aside to dry.

Tint ivory buttercream with a small amount of buttercup yellow to achieve desired shade and ice 2-layer cake smooth. Cover cake top with tip 47 lattice (in a pie crust fashion). Pipe tip 47 shell-motion top and bottom borders. Attach fruit along cake top and bottom border using buttercream icing.

To cherries, add tip 2 stems and tip 349 leaves. To grapes, add tip 2 stems and tip 349 leaves. To bananas, add tip 2 dots to create stems at each end. Serves 10.

Baby Bear

as seen on Page 48

Techniques Needed

Zigzags, Star Fill-in, Ruffles, Zigzag Puffs, Printing, Outline

Wilton Checklist

Pan: Huggable Bear
Tips: 3, 18, 124
Colors: Aster Mauve, Brown
Other: Cake Board, Doilies

Ingredients List

Cake: Prepared 1-Layer Bear
Icing Recipes: Buttercream Icing (2 recipes)

Using a spatula, ice cake sides smooth in white icing, ice bib area smooth in aster mauve icing. Using tip 3 and lt. brown icing, outline bear. Outline and pipe in eyes and nose with tip 3 and dark brown icing; outline mouth. Pipe tip 18 white zigzags for inside ears and pads of paws. Cover body and head with tip 18 light brown stars. Pipe a tip 124 white ruffle around bib and print tip 3 message. Pipe tip 18 zigzag puff bottom border in aster mauve. Serves 12.

Touch of Chocolate

as seen on Page 51

Techniques Needed

Rosettes, Pull-out Stars, Stars, Combing

Wilton Checklist

Pan: 8 x 2 inch Round
Tips: 16, 21, 32
Colors: Brown (optional)
Other: Decorating Triangle, 12 inch Angled Spatula, Cake Circle, cocoa powder, ready-to-spread chocolate fudge icing

Note: To produce mocha icing color shown, mix chocolate fudge icing with buttercream icing or use Brown Icing Color.

Ingredients List

Cake: Prepared 2-Layer Round
Icing Recipes: Buttercream Icing (2 recipes)

Cover 2-layer cake top with white buttercream icing. Use the angled spatula to swirl icing in a spiral pattern. Ice cake sides smooth in lt. mocha colored buttercream and comb using small teeth side of decorating triangle.

Using tip 32 and white buttercream icing, add top and bottom rosette border. Using chocolate fudge icing, add tip 21 pull-out stars to top border rosettes and tip 16 stars to bottom border rosettes. Sprinkle cake top with cocoa. Serves 12.

Sunshine Flourishes

as seen on Page 52 & 65

Techniques Needed

Carnations, Beads, Combing, Ruffles, Leaves

Wilton Checklist

Pan: 8 x 3 inch Round
Tips: 5, 12, 70, 127D, 150
Colors: Buttercup Yellow, Moss Green
Other: Cake Board, 14 inch Featherweight Decorating Bag, Flower Nail #7, Decorating Comb, waxed paper

Ingredients List

Cake: Prepared 1-Layer Round, (torted and filled to 3 inches high)
Icing Recipes: Buttercream Icing (2 recipes), Royal Icing (1 recipe)

Tint royal icing yellow. At least one day in advance, using royal icing on waxed paper and #7 flower nail, make 15 carnations with tip 12 ball base and tip 150 petals. Make extras to allow for breakage. Set aside and let dry.

Tint portions of buttercream icing light buttercup yellow and green. Ice top and sides of cake smooth in yellow buttercream. Use small side of decorating comb to create ridges on cake side. Use 14 inch decorating bag fitted with tip 127D to pipe large ruffle on top edge of cake in white buttercream. Add tip 5 bottom bead border in yellow buttercream. Position carnations and add tip 70 leaves. Serves 10.

Swans Afloat

as seen on Page 57

Techniques Needed

Shell Motion, Leaves, Stems, Ruffles, Lily of the Valley

Wilton Checklist

Pan: 7 x 2 inch Round
Tips: 1, 2, 67, 68, 81
Colors: Ivory, Moss Green
Other: Pearl Swans, Cake Board, Fanci-Foil Wrap

Ingredients List

Cake: Prepared 2-Layer Round, (3 inches high)
Icing Recipes: Buttercream Icing (1 recipe)

Use spatula to ice cake smooth with ivory buttercream icing. Pipe tip 68 leaf top border with green buttercream icing. Randomly pipe lilies of the valley with 68 green elongated leaves, tip 2 green stem and tip 81 white flowers with tip 1 green stamens. Add tip 67 shell motion leaf bottom border (see Shell, page 28) in ivory buttercream icing. Position swans. Serves 10.

Soft Bouquet

as seen on Page 61

Techniques Needed

Wired Flowers, Dots, Leaves, Wild Roses, Reverse Shells, Shells, Leaves

Wilton Checklist

Pan: 8 x 3 inch Round
Tips: 2, 3, 4, 17, 103, 104, 352
Colors: Creamy Peach, Buttercup Yellow, Willow Green, Leaf Green
Other: Meringue Powder, Flower Formers Set, Cake Circles, Decorator Brushes, Flower Nail No. 7, Flower Spikes, green cloth florist's wire, waxed paper

Note: Willow Green and Leaf Green were combined to achieve green color used.

Ingredients List

Cake: Prepared 1-Layer Round, (torted and filled to 3 inches high)
Icing Recipes: Buttercream Icing (1 1/2 recipes), Royal Icing (1 recipe)

At least two days ahead of time use Flower Nail No. 7 and royal icing to make approximately 12 tip 103 white wild roses with tip 2 yellow dot centers and approximately 10-12 tip 104 peach wild roses with tip 2 yellow dot centers. Let flowers dry in flower formers. On four florist's wires, using tip 4 and green royal icing, make 4 bases to attach flowers. Attach 2 white and 2 peach wild roses to wires. Pipe 6 tip 352 green royal icing leaves on florist's wire. Let dry.

Ice 1-layer cake smooth with green buttercream icing. Using green buttercream icing, pipe tip 17 top reverse shell and bottom shell borders. Position flowers on cake and add tip 352 green buttercream leaves. Position wired flowers and leaves in flower spikes before inserting into cake. Serves 10.

Sweet Violets

as seen on Page 62

Techniques Needed

Violets, Dots, Outline

Wilton Checklist

Pan: 7 x 2 inch Round
Tips: 2, 48, 59°
Colors: Violet, Buttercup Yellow
Other: Flower Nail #9, Meringue Powder Mix, Cake Circle, waxed paper, plastic ruler

Ingredients List

Cake: Prepared 2-Layer Round
Icing Recipes: Buttercream Icing (1 1/2 recipes), Royal Icing (1 recipe)

Tint royal icing light and medium violet shades; tint a small amount of icing yellow. Using a flower nail, make approximately 250 tip 59° violets (125 of each violet shade). Add tip 2 yellow dot centers. Make extras to allow for breakage and let dry.

Tint buttercream icing very light violet. Ice 2-layer cake smooth. With a plastic ruler, mark cake sides at 1 inch intervals. Pipe tip 48 vertical lines on each mark. Pipe tip 48 line around bottom border.

Position flowers around bottom border. Using dots of buttercream icing, attach flowers to top edge and top center of cake. Serves 10.

Berry Bonanza

as seen on Page 69

Techniques Needed

Vines, Leaves, Torting

Wilton Checklist

Pan: 8 x 2 inch Round
Tips: 3, 12, 366
Colors: Moss Green, Buttercup Yellow
Other: Red Cake Sparkles (2 pkgs.), Wilton Whipped Topping Mix (1 pkg.), Cake Leveler, rolling pin, raspberry filling, fresh raspberries

Ingredients List

Cake: Prepared 2-Layer Round

Torte each layer in half. Fill layers with raspberry filling, using tip 12 to create a collar of icing, then add filling.

Using whipped topping, spatula ice cake fluffy. Tint whipped topping, combining green and yellow to achieve desired shade. Randomly pipe tip 3 vines over cake. Add tip 366 leaves.

In a resealable plastic bag, crush Cake Sparkles with a rolling pin until very fine. Place several raspberries at a time in bag and shake to coat with sparkles. Position raspberries on cake. Add more raspberries around bottom border. Serves 12.

A Joy to Behold

as seen on Page 71

Techniques Needed

Leaves, Poinsettias, Dots, Balls, Zigzags, Writing

Wilton Checklist

Pan: 9 x 2 inch Round (2 Pan Set)
Tips: 2, 3, 7, 12, 55, 70, 352
Colors: Pink, Moss Green, Buttercup Yellow
Other: Lily Nail Set ($1\frac{5}{8}$ inch nail used), Meringue Powder Mix, Flower Formers Set, Cake Circle, Fanci-Foil Wrap, toothpicks, 3-inch aluminum foil squares, waxed paper, corn syrup

Ingredients List

Cake: Prepared 2-Layer Round
Icing Recipes: Royal, Buttercream Icings (1 recipe each)

Make leaves and flowers at least 1 day ahead of time: Make approximately 75 tip 70 holly leaves. Soften green royal icing by adding 1 teaspoon light corn syrup to each cup of icing used. Pipe leaves one at a time onto squares of waxed paper, then draw leaf ends to a point using a toothpick. Set on flower formers to dry, curving leaves both up and down. Make 8 poinsettias; cake design uses 6, make 2 extras to allow for breakage. Tint royal icing pink for petals and yellow for centers. Position aluminum foil square slightly pushed into $1\frac{5}{8}$ inch lily nail and pipe tip 352 petals with tip 2 center dots. Let dry.

Ice 2-layer cake smooth in white buttercream icing. Using white buttercream icing, pipe a tip 12 zigzag circle on cake top 1 inch in from top edge; pipe tip 7 bottom ball border. Using the zigzag circle as a base, position holly leaves, securing with dots of icing if necessary. Position poinsettias; using pink buttercream, pipe tip 3 dot berries randomly on wreath. Using pink buttercream and tip 55, write message in center of wreath. Serves 22.

Rose Trellis

as seen on Page 72

Techniques Needed

Fondant Roses, Fondant Imprint, Fondant Draping, Dots

Wilton Checklist

Pan: 8 x 3 inch Round
Tip: 2
Color: Buttercup Yellow, Moss Green
Other: Ready-To-Use Rolled Fondant (2 pkgs.), Cake Dividing Set, Easy-Glide Fondant Smoothers, Confectionery Tool Set, Flower Formers Set, Decorator Brush Set, Cake Circles, Floral Collection Flower Making Set

Ingredients List

Cake: Prepared 1-Layer Round
Icing Recipes: Buttercream Icing (1 recipe)

Use 2 packages of Ready-To-Use Rolled Fondant; tint $1\frac{1}{4}$ package yellow, $\frac{1}{2}$ package white and $\frac{1}{4}$ package green. At least one day in advance, make 6 two-tone white and yellow fondant roses using instructions on fondant package. Use leaf cutter from Floral Collection Flower Making Set to cut out approximately 15 green fondant leaves. Use small end of veining tool from Confectionery Tool Set to imprint veins on leaves; let dry on flower formers that have been dusted with cornstarch.

To prepare cake to be covered with yellow fondant, ice with a light layer of buttercream and let set for about 15 minutes. Cover cake with fondant and smooth with Easy-Glide Smoothers. Use Cake Dividing Set to divide cake into 8ths. Roll a length of fondant $\frac{1}{2}$ inch diameter and long enough to wrap around cake. Position around bottom border.

Roll out fondant pieces to be used for drapes: Cut 8 pieces approximately $3\frac{1}{2}$ x 3 inch; pinch and fold to drape. Position drapes at division points of cake; to attach, brush back of drapes with decorator brush dipped in water. Roll out 8 balls of fondant measuring $\frac{3}{8}$ inch diameter. Attach to beginning of each draping point with dots of water.

Pipe tip 2 dots on cake sides above drapes. Attach flowers and leaves to cake top with tip 2 dots of icing. Serves 10.

Love Intertwining

as seen on Page 75

Techniques Needed

Fondant Blossoms, Dots, Fondant Rope

Wilton Checklist

Pan: 9 x 2 inch Heart
Tips: 2
Colors: Aster Mauve, Pink
Other: Cake Circles, Ready-To-Use Rolled Fondant (2 pkgs.), Floral Collection Flower Making Set, Flower Formers Set, Easy-Glide Fondant Smoothers

Ingredients List

Cake: Prepared 2-Layer Heart (3 inches high)
Icing Recipes: Buttercream Icing (1 recipe)

Tint 2 packages of fondant. To achieve color used, combine Aster Mauve and Pink.

One day ahead, make the following flowers using cutters from flower making set: 45 large blossoms using pansy cutter; 20 medium blossoms using apple blossom cutter; 30 small blossoms using forget-me-not cutter. Position flowers on smallest flower former, pipe tip 2 dot centers and let dry.

To prepare 2-layer cake to be covered with mauve/pink fondant, ice with a light layer of buttercream icing and let set for about 15 minutes. Cover cake with fondant and smooth with Easy-Glide Smoothers. Roll 2 pieces of fondant $\frac{1}{2}$ inch diameter, 31 inch long. Twist both pieces into rope and position on bottom border of cake. Attach flowers with tip 2 dots of buttercream icing. Serves 10.

Polka-Dot Party!

as seen on Page 79

Techniques Needed

Fondant Inlay, Beads

Wilton Checklist

Pan: 8 x 2 inch Round
Tips: 8, 8B, 10
Colors: Red-Red, Lemon Yellow, Leaf Green, Royal Blue
Other: Ready-To-Use Rolled Fondant (2 pkgs.), $11\frac{3}{4}$ inch Party Sticks, 26 Pc. Alphabet Cookie Cutter Set, Decorator Brush Set, Easy-Glide Fondant Smoothers, balloons

Ingredients List

Cake: Prepared 2-Layer Round
Icing Recipes: Buttercream Icing (1 recipe)

Prepare 2-layer cake to be covered with fondant using a light layer of buttercream. Use 1 package of white fondant to cover cake and smooth with Easy-Glide Fondant Smoothers. Divide 2nd package into 4ths, tinting $\frac{1}{4}$ red, $\frac{1}{4}$ yellow, $\frac{1}{4}$ green and $\frac{1}{4}$ blue. Use alphabet cookie cutters to cut out name and attach to cake with decorator brush dipped in water.

continued on page 102

Decorating Instructions

Use inlay technique for fondant circles on cake: use large end of tip 8B to cut out and remove circles of fondant on cake; cut same size colored circles and position in cut out areas on cake. Repeat with tip 8 for smaller circles. Position small tinted circles on large tinted circles. Pipe tip 10 bead bottom border.

Attach inflated balloons to party sticks and insert into cake. Serves 12.

A Sweet Present

as seen on Page 82

Techniques Needed

Fondant Bow/Loops
Fondant Ejector Cut-Outs

Wilton Checklist

Pan: 8 x 2 inch Square
Tip: 2
Colors: Teal, Buttercup Yellow, Lemon Yellow
Other: Floral Garland Ejector Set, Ready-To-Use Rolled Fondant (2 pkgs.), Easy-Glide Fondant Smoothers, Decorator Brush Set, Cake Board, ruler

Ingredients List

Cake: Prepared 2-Layer Square (3 inches high)
Icing Recipes: Buttercream Icing (1 recipe)

Tint 1 package Ready-To-Use Rolled Fondant buttercup yellow with a small amount of lemon yellow; tint 1 package teal. At least one day in advance, cut four $8\frac{3}{4}$ x $1\frac{1}{2}$ inch bow loops and one 4 x 2 inch center loop. (Note: Do not cut out ribbon strips ahead of time, they will be placed directly on cake the day the cake is decorated.) Shape each into a loop, pinch ends and stand on side to completely dry. To make flowers, add more buttercup yellow color to a small amount of yellow fondant. Use ejector package directions to make approximately 40 flowers, add tip 2 buttercream dot centers and let dry flat.

To prepare 3-inch cake to be covered with yellow fondant, ice with a light layer of buttercream icing and let set for about 15 minutes. Cover cake with fondant and smooth with Easy-Glide Smoothers. Cut two 15 x $1\frac{1}{2}$ inch ribbon strips in teal fondant. Cut one strip in half. Brush back of ribbon strips with decorator brush dipped in water and attach full strip then half strips to cake. Position bow loops and center loop on cake and attach with brush dipped in water. Attach flowers to bow with tip 2 dots of buttercream icing. Serves 13.

A Warm Welcome

as seen on Page 84

Techniques Needed

Color Flow	Reverse Shells
Stars	Leaves
Vines	Drop Flowers
Writing	

Wilton Checklist

Pan: 9 x 2 inch Round
Tips: 2, 16, 21, 224, 352
Colors: Terra Cotta, Buttercup Yellow, Peach, Royal Blue, Black
Other: Birdhouse and Bird Pattern pg. 103, Parchment Triangles, Color Flow Mix, Meringue Powder, Cake Board, waxed paper

Ingredients List

Cake: Prepared 2-Layer Round
Icing Recipes: Royal Icing ($\frac{1}{2}$ recipe), Buttercream Icing (2 recipes), Color Flow Icing (1 recipe)

Make color flow plaque at least 48 hours ahead of time. Tape birdhouse and bird pattern to work surface; cover with waxed paper and tape in place. With Color Flow Icing Mix in parchment bag fitted with tip 2, outline pattern. (Use the following colors: terra cotta roof, buttercup yellow house, black house opening. gray (small amount of black) post, dark royal blue bird outline, light royal blue body of bird, peach stomach). Let dry 2-3 hours; then flow in remainder of patterns with thinned Color Flow Icing. Let dry. Pipe tip 2 black dot eyes.

At least 1 day ahead of time, using tip 224 and royal icing, make 10 peach drop flowers and 10 buttercup yellow drop flowers, both with tip 2 white dot centers. Let dry.

Using spatula, ice 2-layer cake smooth with white buttercream icing. Edge top border with tip 16 reverse shells and bottom border with alternating tip 21 white and blue stars. Position color flow design* and flowers. Add tip 352 green leaves and tip 2 vines. Write tip 2 message. Serves 22.

**Note: Since buttercream icing will break down color flow, position on a piece of plastic wrap cut to fit, sugar cubes or mini marshmallows.*

Bows All Around!

as seen on Page 88

Techniques Needed

Balls	Outlines
Rosettes	Beads
Sotas	

Wilton Checklist

Pan: 8 x 3 inch Round
Tips: 1, 2, 5, 12
Color: Pink
Other: Crystal-look Bowl, Bow Pattern pg. 103, Cake Board, Cake Dividing Set, Meringue Powder, fresh flowers, waxed paper

Ingredients List

Cake: Prepared 1-Layer Round, (torted and filled to 3 inches high)
Icing Recipes: Buttercream, Royal Icings (1 recipe each)

At least one day in advance, use pattern and royal icing to make 6 bows (make extra in case of breakage): Tape bow pattern to work surface, cover pattern with waxed paper and tape again. Outline pattern with tip 2. Using tip 12 and royal icing, pipe a ball in the center of the bow; add tip 2 rosette on top of ball. Fill in bow with tip 1 sotas. Allow to dry.

Ice top and side of cake smooth with pink buttercream icing. Use tip 5 and pink buttercream icing to pipe bead top and bottom borders. Use Cake Dividing Set to divide cake into 6ths. Attach bows with tip 5 dots of buttercream icing at division points.

Arrange flowers in Crystal-look Bowl, position on cake.Serves 10.

Petit Fours

As seen on page 55

Techniques Needed

Dots	Rosebuds

Wilton Checklist

Pan: Jelly Roll
Tips: 1, 3, 104

Ingredients List

Colors: Creamy Peach, Moss Green
Recipe: Quick-Pour Fondant, Buttercream Icing

Cut cake into $1\frac{1}{4}$ in x $2\frac{1}{2}$ in. rectangles, 2 in. squares, $1\frac{1}{2}$ in. diameter rounds. Tint a portion of fondant lt. peach, reserve a portion white and, following Quick-Pour Fondant recipe, cover cakes with peach and white fondant. Let set.

Tint buttercream icing peach and moss green, reserve a small amount white. Decorate petit fours with tip 104 peach rosebuds with tip 3 green sepals and calyx; add tip 1 white dots. Each serves 1.

Birdhouse and Bird Pattern for "A Warm Welcome" (page 102)

Bow Pattern for "Bows All Around" (page 102)

Wilton Decorating Products

The right tools are essential to great decorating results. On the next ten pages, you'll find some of the most important supplies for any decorator. These unique Wilton products will help you get the most out of your decorating time and talent: bakeware that ensures a quality baked cake, bags and tips that make piping precision shapes easy, icing colors formulated to yield the exact shade you want.

Products are listed with their stock numbers for easy ordering. You can find more great Wilton products in publications such as the annual Wilton Yearbook of Cake Decorating. In addition to a complete product selection, the Yearbook features dozens of exciting cake decorating ideas which use Wilton products.

Bakeware

Wilton has the widest variety of bakeware in the world. More shapes, more sizes in non-stick and anodized aluminum, than anyone. Our selection makes virtually any type of cake possible; our quality construction ensures your cake will turn out beautifully for decorating.

Decorator Preferred®

Wilton's finest bakeware ever! The ultimate bakeware, built with more features to help decorators achieve the best results. Straight sides for perfect 90° corners. A 3-inch depth for more baking versatility. Superior thickness for more consistent baking. A lifetime warranty which ensures you'll enjoy superior construction and performance for a lifetime.

Contours. Rounded top edge, great for rolled fondant.
9 x 3 inch *2105-6121*
3-Pc. Set (7, 11 and 15 inch pans) *2105-6118*
2-Pc. Set (9, 13 inch pans) *2105-6119*

Bevels. Angled edges.
5-Pc. Set (8, 10, 12 inch top bevels, 2 1/2 inch deep; 14 and 16 bottom bevels, 1 1/4 inch deep)...... *2105-6116*
10 inch Top Bevel *2105-6117*

Heating Core. Distributes heat to bake large cakes evenly. ...*417-6100*

Rounds. Each 3 inch deep.
6 inch *2105-6106*
8 inch *2105-6105*
10 inch *2105-6104*
12 inch *2105-6103*
14 inch *2105-6102*
16 inch *2105-6101*
18 inch Half Round *2105-6100*
3-Pc. Sets
(6, 10 and 14 inch) *2105-6114*
(8, 12 and 16 inch) *2105-6115*

Squares
8 inch *2105-6110*
10 inch.......................... *2105-6109*
12 inch.......................... *2105-6108*
14 inch.......................... *2105-6107*

Sheets
9 x 13 inch *2105-6113*
11 x 15 inch *2105-6112*
12 x 18 inch *2105-6111*

Performance Pans™

You can depend on these durable aluminum pans for excellent baking performance, year after year. They will bake cakes with a beautiful light golden surface, ideal for decorating. The classic shapes every decorator needs are here, in a wide range of sizes—rounds and squares from 6 inch to 16 inch diameter. Find Performance Pans at your local Wilton retailer.

Cake Boards & Circles

Strong corrugated cardboard for presenting your cake. For shaped cakes, use pan as a pattern, then cut.

10 x 14 inch 2104-554
13 x 19 inch 2104-552
6 inch diameter 2104-64
8 inch diameter 2104-80
10 inch diameter 2104-102
12 inch diameter 2104-129
14 inch diameter 2104-145
16 inch diameter 2104-160

Professional Turntable

The extra strength and effortless turning pros need for decorating tiered wedding cakes. Heavy-duty aluminum stand, 4⁵/₈ inch high, with 12 inch diameter plate. 307-2501

Trim 'N Turn Cake Stand

Turns smoothly on hidden ball bearings for easy decorating, convenient serving. Flute-edged 12 inch plate. 2103-2518

Featherweight Bags

Use these easy-handling bags over and over again. Lightweight, strong and flexible polyester will never get stiff. Coated to prevent grease from seeping through. May be boiled; dishwasher safe. Instructions included.

8 inch 404-5087
10 inch 404-5109
12 inch 404-5125
14 inch 404-5140
16 inch 404-5168
18 inch 404-5184

Disposable Bags

Use and toss—no fuss, no muss. Perfect for melting Candy Melts® in the microwave, too. Strong, flexible plastic. 12 inch size fits standard tips and couplers.

Pk./12 2104-358
Pk./24 2104-1358

Parchment Triangles

Make your own disposable decorating bags with our grease-resistant vegetable parchment paper.

12 inch Pk./100 2104-1206
15 inch Pk./100 2104-1508

Comfort Grip™ Spatulas

Contoured handles with finger pads for more comfort and control with less fatigue. You will use them for icing cakes, positioning icing flowers, filling decorating bags and performing color striping techniques.

Angled Blade
The perfect angle for icing cake tops.
8 inch 409-6012
13 inch 409-6024
15 inch 409-6036

Straight Blade
Great for icing straight cake sides.
8 inch 409-6006
11 inch 409-6018
15 inch 409-6030

Tapered Blade
Gets to hard-to-reach areas on shaped cakes or cookies.
8 inch 409-6003

Couplers

For easy change of decorating tips on the same icing bag.

Standard

Fits all decorating bags and standard tips. *411-1987*

Angled

Puts your decorating tip in hard-to-reach areas. Fits all bags and standard tips. *411-7365*

Large

Use with large decorating tips and 14 to 18 inch Featherweight Bags. *(See pages 14-15 for details.)*

..................................*411-1006*

Tip Covers

Lets you take filled icing bags along for touch-ups; just slip over the tip and go.

Pk./4 ....*414-915*

Tip Saver

Restores bent tips to their proper shape and opens clogged tips. Place tip over pointed or cone-shaped end, put on cover and twist back and forth to reshape.

.....................................*414-909*

Decorating Comb

Run edge across iced cake to form pretty ridges.

.....................................*417-156*

Decorating Triangle

Each side adds a different contoured effect to iced cakes.

.....................................*417-162*

Flower Former Set

Dry icing leaves and flowers in a convex or concave shape. Includes three each of $1\frac{1}{2}$, 2 and $2\frac{1}{2}$ inch wide holders.

Set/9 ....*417-9500*

Lily Nail Set

Essential for making cup-shaped flowers. Includes $\frac{1}{2}$, $1\frac{1}{2}$, $1\frac{5}{8}$ and $2\frac{1}{2}$ inch diameter cups.

Set/8 ....*403-9444*

Lily Nail

Create beautiful, deep lilies. $1\frac{5}{8}$ inch diameter.

..................................*402-3012*

Flower Nails

Use as "turntables" for piping icing flowers. A variety of sizes—3 inch for large petal tips, 2 inch for curved and swirled petal tips (#118-121), $\frac{1}{2}$ inch No. 7 for basic flower-making, $1\frac{1}{4}$ inch No. 9 for smaller flowers. Stainless steel.

3 inch *402-3003*
2 inch *402-3002*
$1\frac{1}{2}$ inch No. 7 ....*402-3007*
$1\frac{1}{4}$ inch No. 9 ....*402-3009*

Cake Dividing Set

Measures equal sections of your cake for precise placement of garlands and stringwork. Dividing Wheel marks up to 16 divisions on cakes up to 20 inch diameter. Garland Marker adjusts to 7 widths. Instructions included.

Set/2 ....*409-806*

Garland Marker

Adjusts to 7 preset widths and varying depths to easily mark garlands on cake sides. Instructions included.

......................................*409-812*

Pattern Press Sets

Imprint elegant designs for easy overpiping.

Designer Set (purple)
Set/8 ....*2104-3112*

Decorator Favorites Set (teal)
Set/12 ....*2104-3160*

Message Press Sets

Press, then pipe the perfect words. Make-Any-Message Sets include individual letters, others include words or phrases.

All-Occasion Script Message Press Set
Set/8 ....*2104-2090*

Block Letter Press Set
Set/6 ....*2104-2077*

Script Message Press Set
Set/6 ....*2104-2061*

Italic Make-Any-Message Press Set
Set/58 ....*2104-2277*

Make-Any-Message Letter Press Set
Set/56 ....*2104-10*

Alphabet Cookie Cutter Boxed Set

Create letter-perfect cookies, gelatin treats, cheese, sandwiches and more.

Set/26 2304-1521

Step-Saving Rose Bouquet Flower Cutter Set

Create gorgeous gum paste and fondant roses and forget-me-nots using cutters and book in this set.

Set/6 1907-1003

Orchid Bouquet Flower Cutter Set

Make exquisite gum paste and fondant orchids and stephanotis. Cutters and instruction book help you step-by-step.

Set/7 1907-1004

Floral Collection Flower-Making Set

Make incredibly lifelike gum paste flowers. Full-color how-to book includes many arranging ideas and step-by-step instructions. Kit includes 24 plastic cutters, 1 leaf mold, 3 wood modeling tools, protector flap, instruction book, 2 foam squares.

Set/32 1907-117
Book only 907-117

Ready-To-Use Rolled Fondant

No mixing necessary—ready to roll and shape! Covers cakes with a perfectly smooth iced surface. Shape into borders, flowers, decorations. 24 oz. Package covers an 8 inch 2-layer cake plus decorations.

White 710-2076
Chocolate 710-2078

Quick Ease Roller

Makes it easy to prepare small pieces of gum paste and fondant for cutting flowers and designs.

.................................1907-1202

Easy-Glide Fondant Smoothers

Essential tools for shaping and smoothing rolled fondant.

Set/2 1907-1005

Classic Embossing Set

Press stamps into fondant-covered cakes to emboss with elegant designs. Includes ivy leaf, rose, bow, butterfly, bear and heart, complete instructions.

Set/7 1907-1002

Floral Garland Ejector Set

Quickly and easily cuts and positions fondant or gum paste flowers on cakes. Includes ejector, 5 cutters and instructions.

Set/7 1907-1001

Fondant Mold Sets

Just press fondant into molds and release pretty designs to attach to your cake. Great for molded candy too. Includes knife/point tool and instruction book.

Romance Accents Set/3 ...1907-1006
Classic Accents Set/3 1907-1007
Planter Set/3 1907-1009
Baby Accents Set/3 1907-1008

Confectionery Tool Set

Invaluable tools for shaping, imprinting and stenciling—helping you achieve lifelike flowers.Includes Dogbone, Umbrella, Shell, Ball and Veining Tools.

Set/5 1907-1000

Wilton Decorating Products

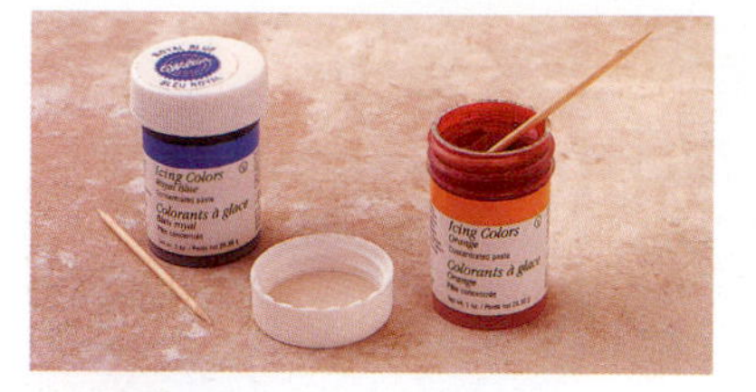

Icing Color

Give your icing the most vivid, realistic color possible with Wilton Icing Colors. Our concentrated gel formula helps you achieve the exact shade you want with only a small amount. You'll find a rainbow of colors, ready to blend together for creating your own custom shades. Certified Kosher. 1 oz.

White-White Color

Stir in to whiten icing made with butter or margarine. Perfect crisp white for wedding cakes.
2 oz. ...*603-1236*

Buttercup Yellow *610-216*
Aster Mauve *610-222*
Delphinium Blue *610-228*
Juniper Green *610-234*
Ivory *610-208*
Black *610-981*
Lemon Yellow *610-108*
Leaf Green *610-809*

Kelly Green *610-752*
Moss Green *610-851*
Teal *610-207*
Sky Blue *610-700*
Violet *610-604*
Daffodil Yellow* *610-175*
Willow Green *610-855*
Cornflower Blue *610-710*

Royal Blue *610-655*
Burgundy *610-698*
Golden Yellow *610-159*
Terra Cotta *610-206*
Christmas Red *610-302*
Copper (Lt. Skintone) *610-450*

Rose Petal Pink *610-410*
Rose *610-401*

Brown *610-507*
Orange *610-205*
Red (No-Taste) *610-998*
Red-Red *610-906*
Creamy Peach *610-210*
Pink *610-256*

Daffodil Yellow is an all-natural color. It does not contain Yellow #5. The color remains very pale.

Ready-To-Use Decorator Icing

Ideal consistency for decorating, flower-making; great for icing cakes too. Just stir and use. 16 oz.

White *710-118*
Chocolate *710-119*

Whipped Icing Mix

Just add ice water and whip up velvety-smooth icing for decorating or covering cakes. Light and delicate flavor. Certified Kosher. Makes 4 cups.

Chocolate *710-1242*
Vanilla *710-1241*

Creamy White Icing Mix

Rich, homemade buttercream taste, great for decorating, add butter and milk. Makes 2 cups.
.....................................*710-112*

Meringue Powder

Used for royal icing, meringue, boiled icing; stabilizes buttercream. Replaces egg white in some recipes. Resealable top opens completely for easy measuring. Certified Kosher.

4 oz. can *702-6007*
8 oz. can *702-6015*

Color Flow Mix

Create dimensional flow-in designs for your cake. Just add water and confectioners' sugar. 4 oz. can makes ten $1^1/2$ cup batches. Certified Kosher.

4 oz. can *701-47*

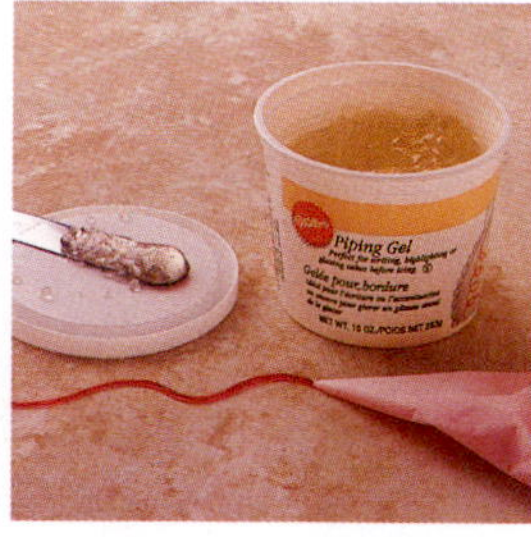

Piping Gel

Clear icing gel makes shimmering designs and messages, or glazes cakes before icing. Tint with icing color. Certified Kosher.

10 oz. *704-105*

Glycerin

Stir into dried out icing color to restore consistency. Certified Kosher.

2 oz. *708-14*

Flavors/Extracts

Ideal for decorating, no-color flavors and extracts won't change icing color. Certified Kosher.

Butter Flavor
2 oz. *604-2040*
8 oz. *604-2067*
Vanilla Extract
2 oz. *604-2237*
8 oz. *604-2269*
Almond Extract
2 oz. *604-2126*

Colored Sugar

Extra-fine sugars in flip-top shaker bottles are excellent for filling in designs on cakes, cookies, cupcakes. 3 oz.

Light Green *710-752*	Lavender *710-758*	Dark Green *710-764*
Yellow *710-754*	Orange *710-759*	Red *710-766*
Pink *710-756*	Black *710-762*	Blue *710-750*

Cake Sparkles™

Brilliant edible glitter adds shimmering color to your desserts. Great for stenciling, borders, flowers, snow scenes. Certified Kosher. 1/4 oz.

White *703-1290*	Light Blue *703-1262*	Black *703-1302*	Rainbow *703-1296*
Purple *703-1266*	Green *703-1278*	Red *703-1284*	Blue *703-1314*
Pink *703-1260*	Orange *703-1308*	Yellow *703-1272*	Brown *703-1320*

Decorator's Sets

Starter Set

A good assortment to create Wilton character cakes. 18 pc. set includes four tips, six disposable decorating bags, two couplers, five color packets, booklet.

.................................*2104-2530*

Basic Set

A solid foundation for decorating star fill-in birthday designs to floral cakes. 25 pc. set includes five tips, twelve disposable decorating bags, two couplers, four color packets, flower nail, booklet.

.................................*2104-2536*

Deluxe Set

Ideal for advanced floral cakes and basic wedding designs. 37 pc. set includes ten tips, eighteen disposable bags, two couplers, four colors, flower nail, storage tray, book.

.................................*2104-2540*

Supreme Set

Decorate many advanced wedding, floral and basketweave designs. 53 pc. set includes eighteen tips, twenty-four disposable decorating bags, two couplers, five colors, flower nail, angled spatula, storage tray, book.

.................................*2104-2546*

Deluxe Tip Set

Create basic and advanced borders, flower s and more. 26 metal tips, tip coupler, flower nail, plastic tipsaver case.

.................................*2104-6666*

Master Tip Set

The ultimate set for virtually any technique. 52 metal tips, tip couplers, two flower nails, plastic tipsaver case.

.................................*2104-7778*

Tool Caddy

Lift-out tray holds tips and colors upright for easy viewing. Generous storage area under tray for spatulas, books, bags, more. Tips, colors not included. ...*409-860*

Decorating Tips

For decades, Wilton Decorating Tips have set the standard. And the selection is unsurpassed—there are hundreds to choose from!

Constructed of rust-resistant, durable nickel-plated brass, Wilton decorating tips keep their shape and produce precise designs year after year. Many decorators keep multiple tips of their-most used and liked tips on hand. This makes decorating much quicker and easier—no need to stop decorating to clean a new tip for use.

The next four pages profile many of the most-popular Wilton Decorating Tips. Take a look, choose your favorites!

Round Tips

Extra Small
For fine cornelli lace, icing embroidery, fine stringwork.

Small
For scrolls, vines, stems, flower centers, cornelli lace, stringwork, filigree, lattice, script, dots, lace pieces, outlines.

Medium
For bead borders, dots, scrolls, outlines, flower centers, rose bases, figure piping.

Large
For figure piping, icing bases, wedding cake bead borders.

Oval
For Philippine method flower-making, lettering.

Tip No.	Stock No.
Extra Small	
1s	402-1009
1L	402-901
Small	
1	402-1
2	402-2
3	402-3
4	402-4
Medium	
5	402-5
6	402-6
7	402-7
8	402-8
9	402-9
10	402-10
11	402-11
12	402-12
Large	
1A	402-1001
2A	402-2001
Oval	
55	402-55
57	402-57
301	402-301

Multi-String Tips

Multiple Line
42 triple strings.
89 For twin line stringwork, garlands, zigzag, lattice.

Musical Scale
For five string musical scale design.

Multi-Hole
For hair and grass on novelty cakes. Tiny holes make spaghetti-like strings with one squeeze.

Tip No.	Stock No.
Multiple Line	
42	402-42
89	402-89
Musical Scale	
134	402-134
Multi-Hole	
233	402-233
234	402-234
235	402-235

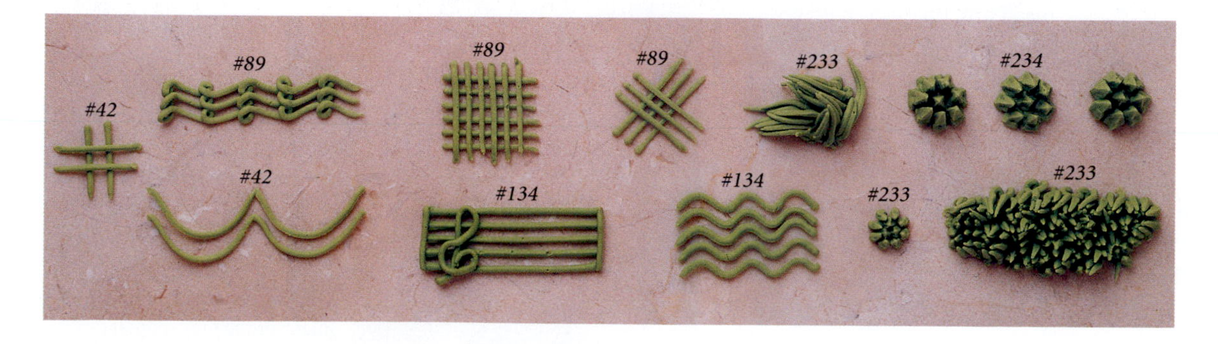

Tip No.	Stock No.
Deep Star Open	
13	402-13
14	402-14
15	402-15
16	402-16
17	402-17
18	402-18
19	402-19
20	402-20
21	402-21
22	402-22
2010 (3 star)	402-2010
2110 (1M)	402-2110
Deep Star Closed	
24	402-24
26	402-26
27	402-27
28	402-28
29	402-29
30	402-30
31	402-31
133	402-133
195	402-195
Standard Cut Open	
32	402-32
96	402-96
4B	402-4400
6B	402-6600
8B	402-8800
Fine Cut	
172	402-172
199	402-199
362	402-362
363	402-363
364	402-364
Deep Cut Stellar	
501, 502, 504, 506, 508 set/5	402-502

Deep Star Open
For stars, shells, puffs, rosettes, baby's breath, zigzags, stripes, scrolls, fleurs-de-lis, garlands, drop flowers, ropes.

Deep Star Closed
For sharply ribbed decorations. For rosettes, stars, shells, fleurs-de-lis, drop flowers, scrolls.

Standard Cut Open
For shells, scrolls, figure piping, zigzags, stars, puffs.

Fine Cut
For shells and puffs with many ridges. Beautiful on rolled fondant covered cakes and with Lambeth decorating method.

Deep Cut Stellar
For lavish shells, scrolls, flowers in perfect proportion to cake tiers. Tip series ideal for wedding cake borders.

Drop Flower Tips

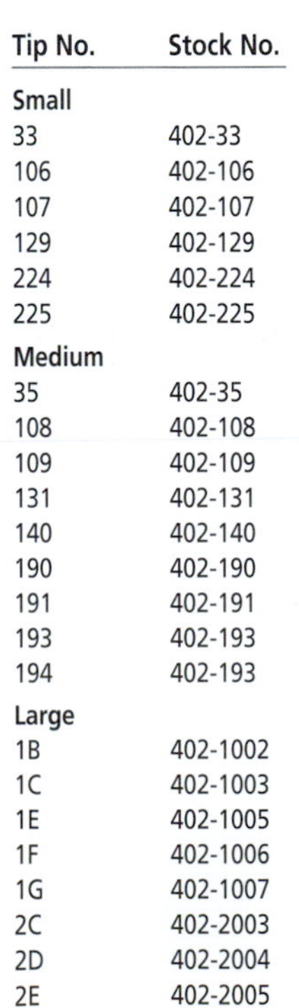

Tip No.	Stock No.
Small	
33	402-33
106	402-106
107	402-107
129	402-129
224	402-224
225	402-225
Medium	
35	402-35
108	402-108
109	402-109
131	402-131
140	402-140
190	402-190
191	402-191
193	402-193
194	402-193
Large	
1B	402-1002
1C	402-1003
1E	402-1005
1F	402-1006
1G	402-1007
2C	402-2003
2D	402-2004
2E	402-2005
2F	402-2006

Small
For star or swirl flowers.

Medium
For bigger star or swirl flowers.

Large
For large flowers as cake accents and on floral sprays. Single and double petals.

Rose Tips

Plain

101s, 101, 102, 103, 104, 124, 125, 126, *127* For roses, sweet peas, pansies, rose-buds, daisies, daffodils, ruffles, bows, more.
127D Giant Rose Tip

Swirled

For curvier, lifelike roses and buds with instant-curled petals. For curvy ribbon zigzags.

Curved

For violets, pansies, zigzags, narcissi, ribbon swags, drapes.

Cut

For zigzag and "e" motion borders, half smooth and half ridged ribbon bows, swags, drapes.

Carnation

For lifelike carnations with ruffled edges.

Tip No.	Stock No.
Plain	
101s	402-1019
101	402-101
102	402-102
103	402-103
104	402-104
124	402-124
125	402-125
126	402-126
127	402-127
127D	402-1274
Swirled	
97	402-97
116	402-116
Curved	
59s/59°	402-594
59	402-59
60	402-60
61	402-61
121	402-121
123	402-123
Cut	
62	402-62
64	402-64
Carnation	
150	402-150

Leaf Tips

Plain Cut

65s, 65, 66, 67, 68, 69, 70 small
112, 113, 115 extra large For natural-looking leaf with center vein and for wide leaves, ferns, borders.

Special Cut

For lilies, poinsettias, dahlias, ferns, Christmas tree and wreath leaves and stand-up leaves using tree formers. For shell border, garlands.

V-Cut

Large ***326, 352***
Small ***349, 366***
For never-fail pointed leaves,ferns.

Tip No.	Stock No.
Plain Cut	
65s	402-659
65	402-65
66	402-66
67	402-67
68	402-68
69	402-69
70	402-70
112	402-112
113	402-113
115	402-115
Special Cut	
73	402-73
74	402-74
75	402-75
V-Cut	
326	402-326
349	402-349
352	402-352
366	402-366

Specialty Tips

Tip No.	Stock No.
Fluted	
79	402-79
80	402-80
81	402-81
Cross	
54	402-54
96	402-96
77	402-77
78	402-78
Square	
83	402-83
Miscellaneous	
105	402-105
136	402-136
230	402-230
250	402-250
252	402-252
Special Border	
98	402-98

Fluted
For blossoms, lily-of-the-valley, zigzags, mums, "e" motion borders.

Cross
54, 96 Shells, fancy effects
77, 78 For buds, ornate line work, small 4-petal drop flowers.

Square
For sculptured, 3-dimensional printing, outlines, beads, zigzag, "e" motion borders.

Miscellaneous
105, 347 For shells, ropes, basketweave, more.
250 Tree.
252 Heart.
230 Bismarck Filler
136 Makes icing ring candle holders.

Special Border
For richly-puffed shells and garlands.

Basketweave Tips

Tip No.	Stock No.
Small/Medium	
44	402-44
45	402-45
46	402-46
47	402-47
48	402-48
Large	
1D	402-1004
2B	402-2002
Extra Large	
789	409-789

Small/Medium
46, 47 For ribbed or smooth ribbons, basketweaves, stripes, bows.
44, 45 smooth stripes.
48 ribbed stripes.

Large
For wide, smooth or ribbed shell borders, stripes, basketweaves.

Extra Large
For icing cake top and sides with extra-wide smooth or ribbed stripes.

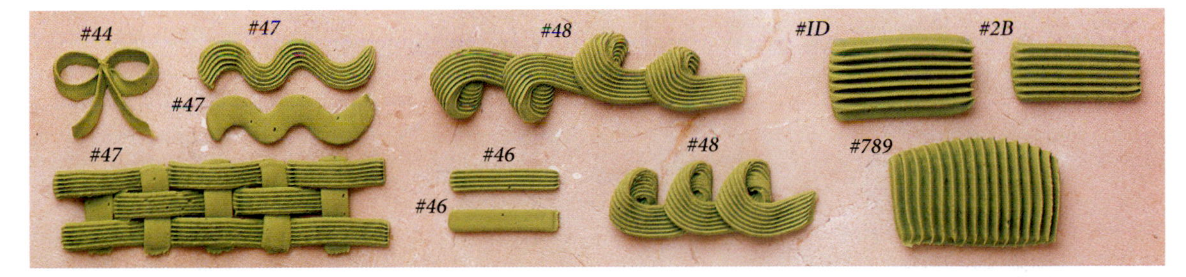

Ruffle Tips

Tip No.	Stock No.
Double Ribbon	
100	402-100
340	402-340
Star Cut	
86	402-86
87	402-87
88	402-88
95	402-95
Ripple Ribbon	
353	402-353
401	402-401
402	402-402
403	402-403
406	402-406

Double Ribbon
For double fluted ruffles.

Star Cut
95 deeply-grooved french leaf borders
86, 87, 88 For shell and flute border in one step (lefties use 87, 88).

Ripple Ribbon
For extra-wide zigzag borders, ears, tongues and feathers on novelty cakes.

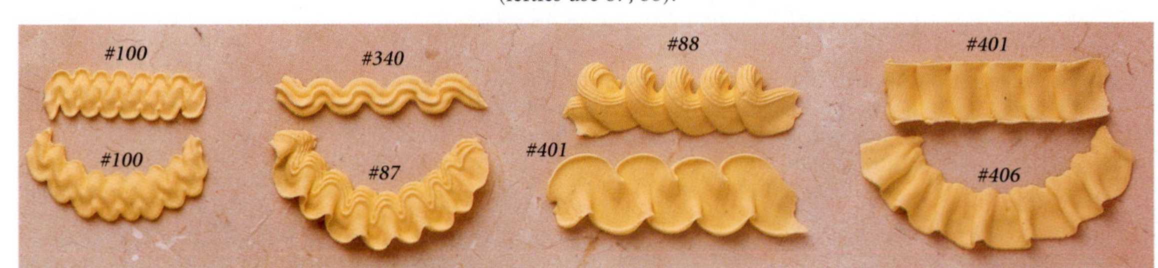

Glossary of Terms

Attach
To secure icing decorations to cake using dots of icing. Use your icing to attach as you would use "glue".

Basketweave
Technique using a decorating tip making stripes and producing an interwoven effect.

Border
A continuous decoration used around the top, side or base of a cake.

Brush Striping
Applying one or more stripes of icing color with a decorator brush to the inside of a parchment bag, then filling the bag with white or colored icing to produce multi-colored decorations.

Buttercream Icing
All-purpose decorating icing made of sugar, shortening and flavoring that is good tasting and easy to work with.

Cake Circle
Corrugated cardboard rounds sized to provide bases for standard circular and shaped cakes.

Calyx
The cuplike green portion of the flowers connecting the petals to the stem.

Color Flow Icing Mix
An egg white based powder that produces Color Flow icing when mixed with water and confectioners' sugar.

Coupler
A grooved insert and retainer ring. When used with a decorating bag allows tip changing without changing decorating bags. The coupler has two parts: the inner coupler base and the outer coupler ring.

Decorating Bag
The container that holds your decorating tip and decorating icing. Bags can be made from plastic or parchment paper.

Decorating Tips
Specially-shaped, open-end metal tips used to form icing decorations.

Decorator Brush
A small brush used to smooth icing, paint details and add color to decorating bags.

Dowel Rods
Wooden or plastic supports used to reinforce cake tiers.

Elongate
To lengthen a decoration beyond its usual size. To elongate a technique, such as a star or shell, keep an even pressure, pull smoothly to desired length, then release pressure and stop squeezing bag.

Note: Specific product information pertains only to Wilton products.

Featherweight Bag
Reusable polyester coated decorating bag.

Figure Piping
Decorating technique used to form figures out of icing.

Filling
Icing, preserves or pudding between cake layers to hold them together and add more flavor.

Flower Former
A curved plastic decorating aid used to dry Royal icing flowers, curved petals and leaves for a more natural, curved shape.

Flower Nail
Round, flat surfaced metal tool used as a base on which to make different icing flowers.

Garland
A draped cake decoration made of icing and used as a border. It is heavier in the middle than at sides and is done scalloped, zigzag, puff or as stringwork.

Glucose
Used in gum paste and candy making. Wilton Glucose is made from corn syrup that has not come into contact with animal sources, and is Kosher.

Glycerin
Used to restore consistency to dried icing colors and in fondant icing. Wilton Glycerin is synthetic and Kosher.

Icing
A mixture of sugar, butter, and flavorings used to cover a cake and from which decorative, edible designs are created.

Icing Color
Concentrated product used for adding color to icing and other foods.

Lacework
A delicate cake decorating technique often applied to wedding, shower and fondant-covered cakes.

Latticework
Crossed stripes of icing with openings between them.

Leveling
Removing the rounded top portion, or "crown" of a cake to provide a flat surface for icing and decorating.

Meringue Powder
Product made with pasteurized dried egg whites and cornstarch; used to make hard-drying royal icing. Safe to use in icings, meringue and mousses. Also adds strength to sugar molds and stabilizes buttercream icing.

Outline or Strings
Icing that flows out of the tip to follow contours of a shaped cake or to cover pattern design marks.

Parchment Bag
Disposable decorating bags formed from parchment paper triangles.

Pillars
Columns used with separator plates to support and separate tiers of cake.

Piping
Squeezing icing out of a bag to form decoration.

Piping Gel
Transparent gel that can be tinted any color for decorating or writing.

Poured Fondant Icing
A sweet, pourable icing that dries to a shiny, smooth surface. Used to coat cakes, petit fours and cookies.

Rolled Fondant Icing
Sweet, dough-like consistency icing used for covering cakes and making decorations.

Royal Icing
Smooth, hard-drying icing for decorations that last indefinitely, ideal for flowers and trims made in advance.

Score
Using your spatula edge to make a mark in icing by gently pressing it against the surface.

Sepal
The individual green leaves covering the base of the flower and extending up the calyx.

Separator Plates
Plastic supporting plates for tiered cakes.

Spatula Striping
Adding a stripe of colored icing to the inside of a decorating bag, then filling the bag with a second color icing to produce two-tone decorations.

Stabilize
To maintain a texture or prevent separation, as in adding piping gel to whipped cream or meringue powder to buttercream icing.

Stamen
One of the reproductive parts of a flower usually found in the center of the flower.

Stringwork
Loops of icing draped around the side of the cake.

Sugar Mold
A decorative shape made from a mixture of granulated sugar with a small amount of water, molded and allowed to dry completely. Also refers to the mold or container in which the sugar mixture is packed and formed.

Tiered Cake
A combination of two or more cakes stacked on top of one another.

Torting
Splitting a single cake layer in half horizontally to form two layers.

Index

Keeping In Touch With Wilton

There's always something new at Wilton! Fun decorating courses that will help your decorating skills soar. Exciting cake designs to challenge you. Great new decorating products to try. Helpful hints to make your decorating more efficient and successful. Here's how you can keep up to date with what's happening at Wilton.

Decorating Classes

Do you want to learn more about cake decorating, with the personal guidance of a Wilton instructor? Wilton has two ways to help you.

The Wilton School of Cake Decorating is where the decorating techniques in this book began. During more than half a century, thousands of students from around the world have learned to decorate cakes with The Wilton Method. In 1929, Dewey McKinley Wilton taught the first small classes in the kitchen of his Chicago home. Today, The Wilton School teaches more people to decorate than any school in the world. As the school has grown, some techniques have been refined and there are more classes to choose from—but the main philosophies of the Wilton Method have remained.

The Wilton School now occupies a new state-of-the-art facility in Darien, Illinois. More than 20 courses are offered each year, including The Master Course, a 2-week class that provides individualized instruction in everything from borders and flowers to constructing a tiered wedding cake. Other courses focus on specific decorating subjects, such as Lambeth and Cakes for Catering. Courses in Gum Paste and Chocolate Artistry feature personal instruction from well-known experts in the field.

For more information or to enroll, write to:
School Secretary, Wilton School of Cake Decorating and Confectionery Art
2240 West 75th Street, Woodridge, IL 60517

Or call: 630-810-2211
For free brochure and schedule

Wilton Class Programs are the convenient way to learn to decorate, close to your home. Our Wilton Method Classes are easy and fun for everyone. You can learn the fundamentals of cake decorating with a Wilton-trained teacher in just four 2-hour classes. When the course is over, you'll know how to decorate star and shell birthday cakes or floral anniversary cakes like a pro. Everyone has a good time—it's a great place for new decorators to discover their talent. Since 1974, hundreds of thousands have enjoyed these courses. Special Project Classes are also available in subjects like candy-making, gingerbread, fondant, cookie blossoms and more.

Call 800-942-8881 for class locations and schedules.

Wilton Products

Visit a Wilton Dealer near you. Your local Wilton Dealer is the best place to see the great variety of cake decorating products made by Wilton. If you are new to decorating, it's a good idea to see these products in person; if you are an experienced decorator, you'll want to visit your Wilton Dealer regularly to have the supplies you need on hand. From bakeware and icing supplies to candles and publications, most Wilton retailers carry a good stock of items needed for decorating. Remember, the selection of products changes with each season, so if you want to decorate cakes in time for upcoming holidays, visit often to stock up on current pans, colors and toppers.

You may also call 800-794-5866 (7WILTON) to place an order. Or, you can place orders at our website, *www.wilton.com,* and by mail, using the Order Form in the Wilton Yearbook of Cake Decorating.

Wilton On The Web

www.wilton.com is the place to find Wilton decorating information on-line. Looking for a fun new cake to make? Our website is filled with great decorating ideas, updated regularly to fit the season. Need a recipe? *www.wilton.com* has delicious desserts and icings to try. Want to save decorating time? There are always helpful hints and answers to common decorating questions. You can also discover new Wilton products and shop for your favorites at *www.wilton.com.*

Wilton Publications

We never run out of decorating ideas! Each year, Wilton publishes several new idea books based on Wilton Method techniques. When you're planning a special occasion, Wilton books are a fantastic source of decorating inspiration.

The Wilton Yearbook of Cake Decorating is our annual showcase of the latest ideas in decorating. Each edition is packed with all-new cake ideas, instructions and products—it's the best place to find out what's new at Wilton. Cakes for every occasion throughout the year are here: holidays, graduations, birthdays, weddings and more. If you're looking for a new cake to test your decorating skills, you can't beat the Yearbook.

Wilton also regularly publishes special interest decorating books, including books on wedding and holiday decorating, candy-making, home entertaining and food gifting. Look for them wherever Wilton products are sold.